ENGLISH NIGHT-LIFE

FROM NORMAN CURFEW TO
PRESENT BLACK-OUT

By
THOMAS BURKE

*Illustrated from
Prints, Paintings, Drawings and Photographs*

Copyright © 2013 Read Books Ltd.
This book is copyright and may not be
reproduced or copied in any way without
the express permission of the publisher in writing

British Library Cataloguing-in-Publication Data
A catalogue record for this book is available from the
British Library

Thomas Burke

Thomas Burke was born in Clapham, London in 1886. His father died when he was very young, and at the age of ten he was removed to a home for middle-class boys who were "respectably descended but without adequate means to their support." Burke published his first piece of writing – a short story entitled 'The Bellamy Diamonds' – in 1901, when he was just fifteen. However, proper recognition came in 1916, with the publication of *Limehouse Nights,* a collection of melodramatic short stories set amongst the immigrant population of London's Chinatown. *Limehouse Nights* was serialized in three British periodicals, *The English Review, Colour* and *The New Witness,* and received positive attention from reviewers and a number of authors, including H. G. Wells. It also sparked something of a controversy, however, and was initially banned by libraries due to the scandalous interracial relationships it portrayed between Chinese men and white women.

It was these portrayals of London's Chinatown that Burke is best-remembered for. However, there is some degree of confusion over how much of Burke's writing was based in fact; as literary critic Anne Witchard states, most of what we know about Burke's life is based on works that "purport to be autobiographical, yet contain far more invention than truth." Whatever the truth, there is no doubt that, in his day, Burke was regarded as the foremost chronicler of London's Chinatown at the turn-of-the-century. Burke told newspaper journalists that he had "sat at the feet of Chinese philosophers who kept opium dens to learn from the lips that could frame only broken English, the secrets, good and evil, of the mysterious East," and these journalists almost uniformly took him at his word.

Burke continued to use descriptions of urban London life as a focus of his writing throughout his life. Off the back of *Limehouse Nights,* Burke published the thematically similar *Twinkletoes* in 1918, and *More Limehouse Nights* in 1921. However, he was a prolific author who tried his hand at a number of different genres. He semi-regularly published essays on the London environment, including pieces such as 'The Real East End' and 'London in My Times', and during the thirties even tried his hand at horror fiction. Indeed, in 1949, shortly after his death, Burke's short story 'The Hands of Ottermole' was voted the best mystery of all time by critics. Burke also influenced the burgeoning film industry in Hollywood; D W Griffith, for example, used the short story 'The Chink and the Child' from *Limehouse Nights* (1917) as basis for his silent movie, *Broken Blossoms* (1919), and Charlie Chaplin derived 'A Dog's Life' (1918) from the same book.

1 The Return from the Tythe Feast (1829)

By the Same Author

THE STREETS OF LONDON
THROUGH THE CENTURIES

152 pages of text, 2 Colour Plates, and over 100 reproductions from prints, drawings, paintings and photographs.

Demy 8vo.   10s. 6d. net

"... An entertaining and skilfully-handled sketch of London life through the centuries, very varied and many-sided ... the illustrations are well chosen." — *The Spectator*

"... This beautifully produced and richly illustrated volume ... is a mine of out-of-the-way facts." — *The Daily Telegraph*

"... A variety of ingredients have been mixed together in *The Streets of London*. Smollett's prose and Hogarth's paint; Rowlandson and Cruikshank and Pepys; 'Nollekens' Smith's engravings of London beggars; photograph and medieval tailpiece; doggerel and ballad—with the cement of Mr. Burke's narrative, they make a lively and original London miscellany." — *The New Statesman and Nation*

Published by
B. T. BATSFORD LTD.
15 North Audley Street, London, W.1

Preface

NIGHT-LIFE . . . Night-club . . . Night-bird. There is something about the word Night, as about the word Paris, that sends through some Englishmen a shiver of misgiving, and through another type a current of undue delight. The latter never get over the excitement of Sitting Up Late. The others see any happening after midnight—even a game of snakes-and-ladders—as something verging on the unholy; as though Satan were never abroad in sunlight. A club they can tolerate. Call it a night-club, and they see it as the ante-room to hell.

This attitude towards entertainment after dark is held by most officials. Whenever they hear of some new development of night-life, they get a pricking of the thumbs, and give the impression that they would be happier if the universe had so contrived its system as to give the whole globe perpetual day. They always want to have their eye on us; always are ordering their subordinates to find out what baby is doing and tell him he mustn't.

This impeding of the Englishman's night-life goes back to our earliest times, and has persisted ever since. In my own youth a firm of billiards-table makers used to recommend its wares to respectable fathers, under the legend: Keep Your Boys At Home. But all through the centuries boys have refused to stay at home. So, when authority found that it could not keep them there, it set about making things as difficult as possible for them by devising budgets of laws and bye-laws. Even the English theatre existed only by official grace. It was—and still is—hampered by many laws out of key with the spirit of the time. Even to-day the free and enlightened Englishman may not see a play till it has been scrutinized and purged by a Government official or a local Watch Committee.

But despite restrictions, the spirit of the old anthem of Night-Life, the Won't-Go-Home-Till-Morning spirit, was never extinguished. That anthem, set to the air of *Malbrouck s'en va-t-en guerre*, was at once a demand for applause of devilry, and a challenge. I can't discover the author of that verse, but whoever he was, he did something that is as much a part of our national song as *Rule, Britannia*. It might be called A Song Against All Parents, Guardians, and Town Councillors. The spirit it expresses belongs to all periods of our history. It is with us even in these dark days, though there is, just now, little substance to it—at least, in the large cities. Those who have always frowned upon any all-night night-life must, for once in their lives, be content. Night-clubs and supper-and-dance clubs carry on in a rather brittle way, and some amusement after the theatre may still be had; but it is necessarily of a tepid kind.

Still, while most of the amenities of life have, under the present stress, been cheerfully surrendered for a while, we may still remember what was. If we haven't much night-life to-day, and are in no true mood for it, we may still find a poor and tantalizing substitute in reading about it. In the chapters that follow I have attempted to show something of all aspects of English night-life through some six hundred years. One or two reviewers of another book of mine in this series, *The Streets of London*, complained that both text and illustrations were rather weighted on the side of the shady and the riotous. They may be inclined to make the same complaint of this book. But what is one to do? In writing on these subjects, one is dependent upon contemporary authorities. And both authors and artists of any particular period are apt to find their material in the more ebullient expressions of life. Quiet people going quietly about their occasions do not afford very fruitful material for either pen or pencil. We know they were there, and that their quiet ways and seemly life, whether in the streets of London or in the night-resorts of England, were a regular part of the social scene and were typical of the majority. But we find precious little account of them. They were taken for granted, and authors and artists selected their episodes and scenes from the unusual and the fantastic; even the grotesque.

Anyway, here is a little record of English night-life drawn from many sources. It may evoke some exasperated regret in the minds of those sitting behind drawn and sealed curtains, or fumbling and stumbling from a shrouded restaurant into streets darker than those of Elizabethan England. But some time or other the German Fury will be in chains, and the lights will go up, and our minds and spirits will go up. Civilization and intelligence will again brighten our days and nights, and those who brought the darkness upon the world will themselves be in it.

T. B.

LONDON, *October, 1941*

Acknowledgment

THE publishers must express a special debt of gratitude to Messrs. Walter T. Spencer, of New Oxford Street, from whose magnificent collection of prints and books so many of the illustrations have been taken. Most of the remainder are from public or private collections, including those of the author and the publishers. Figs. 17, 37 and 60 are from originals in the Victoria and Albert Museum, and Figs. 66 and 67 are reproduced by special permission of the Proprietors of *Punch*. Of the photographs, the publishers are indebted to Dorien Leigh, Ltd., for Figs. 68, 72, 73, 75, 76, 77 and 79; Fox Photos, for Figs. 71, 74 and 81; General Photographic Agency, for Figs. 69 and 78; Keystone View Co., for Fig. 80; and Wide World Photos, for Fig. 70.

Contents

	Page
PREFACE	v
ACKNOWLEDGMENT	vii
EARLY TO BED	1
NIGHT INTO DAY	23
WE WON'T GO HOME TILL MORNING	71
NIGHTS OF OUR OWN TIME	133
INDEX	145

Early to Bed

"Lord! What good hours do we keep!"

NIGHT-LIFE IN ENGLAND. . . . If night-life means, as it does with most people, relaxation and festivity, then scarcely any city or town of England, at the time of writing, has any open and general night-life to enjoy. And at this time, 1941, only a prophet careless of the ancient and honoured fame of prophecy would dare to name a time when really light-hearted revelry will again rejoice the midnight hours.

We have grown so accustomed to some form of evening and midnight life that many of us think that in living without our late theatres, balls and receptions, we are making social history. We are, of course, only repeating it. Manners and customs move always in circles, and in these war-years we have put ourselves back among the conditions prevailing in very old England. In that old England night-life was not a feature of the social scene. For many centuries from the time of the Conquest it could not be. At any time its first requirement has been, both as background and garnish, bright lights; and they had then, by lack of means, no more bright lights than we have to-day by lack of peace.

Nor was that its only impediment. Authority itself was against it. The sheriffs and city fathers throughout England regarded the hours of darkness as hours fit only for deeds of darkness. Night was synonymous with evil, with conspiracies and stratagems, and they made it so. The city or town gates were closed at sunset; taverns had to close at eight or nine o'clock; and thereafter the city or town was (officially) dead until daybreak. To be abroad at midnight without very good reason—such as carrying an urgent summons to a midwife or seeking a chirurgeon—was a crime. The law, of course, like every law, was frequently broken, not only by thieves and marauders, but by the young and spirited, like the son of Henry IV and the young Shallow, who were impatient of confinement and determined, law or no law, to be companions to the chimes at midnight. But then, if a law is not going to be broken there is no occasion for making it. The lower kind of tavern kept open at will, with bribes to the watch. The gaming-rooms kept open for a twenty-four hour service. And there were, of course, in every town, the houses of assignation which, when they were most closely shuttered, were most open.

But by the majority of people the law was strictly observed because it was in harmony with their own habits. The rule in those days, for both gentle and simple, was Early to Bed, Early to Rise. In summer, as Nicolas Breton's *Fantastickes* shows, town as well as country was up and doing at five in the morning; in winter, at seven:

> *The Fifth Hour.* Fie sluggards that would be asleep; the bells ring to prayer, and the streets are full of people, and the highways stored with travellers. The scholars are up and going to school. . . . The blind fiddler is up with his dance and his song, and the ale-house door is unlocked for good fellows.

At ten o'clock preparations were being made for dinner, and at eleven o'clock dinner was served and the minstrels waited at the doors of the rich to be ready with their after-dinner music. Dinner, and the wine that succeeded, kept the company at table till two o'clock. Traders and merchants continued their affairs during the afternoon, and closed them, in summer, at twilight, and in winter at dark. This was not only dictated (as in 1941) by general conditions; in some trades it was enforced by their Guilds, which had a rule that no member should sell his goods by candle-light, thus avoiding any possible temptation to use the advantage of poor light (as some stall-holders did) to foist inferior goods on the buyer. Supper was at six, and in summer was followed by a walk to the fields round about, where the young could enjoy spontaneous dancing or other physical sports while the elders gossiped. But in winter-time supper, for the majority, was followed soon after by bed.

Night-life under artificial light, in those early days, affords therefore little matter for comment; no more indeed than the mythical author of *The Fauna of Iceland* made in his chapter on Snakes. Such nocturnal entertainment as happened was private and domestic, and it happened only in the mansions and halls of the noble and the wealthy. They had their hired minstrels, their masques and mummers and dances—the Brawl, the Galliard, the Lavolta, the Hey; and they had their own lutes or citherns, their theorbos or virginals, and their card or table games.

In the halls of old castles and manor-houses one may still see the minstrels' gallery, where, after the household dinner or supper, to which servants as well as family sat down, entertainment was given by harpists, gleemen, jongleurs and mummers. In cities and towns, the mansions of the rich merchants and the lords all had their great hall and their galleries, and some kind of entertainment was provided each night:

> Come now; what masques, what dances shall we have,
> To wear away this long age of three hours
> Between our after-supper and bed-time?
> Where is our usual manager of mirth?
> What revels are in hand? Is there no play
> To ease the anguish of a torturing hour?

2 A Court Soirée in the Fifteenth Century

3 An Accident at a Fifteenth-century Entertainment: the Mummers catch Fire!

4 Cardinal Wolsey holds a Banquet in the Presence Chamber at Hampton Court
A reconstruction by Joseph Nash

The masques and revels and pageants of the Court and the great houses were produced as sumptuously and with as little regard for cost as the twentieth-century shows of the film companies. They were specially written and devised by masters in the art, and the music was entrusted to the leading melodist of the day. Scenery and costumes were designed by artists, and everything was done on a far more elaborate and cloth-of-gold scale than was used in the theatres which came later, in the 1570's. The masque was not so much a play as an amateur entertainment based on some poetic legend—usually classical or allegorical—and broken with songs and processions. The performers often numbered some hundreds, and principal parts were sometimes taken by ladies of the Court or members of the household in which the masque was given.

A feature of the early days of travel was the entertainment offered to the wayfarer at his inn. At supper the "town music" would wait upon him; and after supper there would be perhaps the wandering fiddler, the ballad-singer, the juggler, or the travelling showman with his "motions," who would be allowed to lie in the barn without charge in return for giving the guests a show. These private entertainments were for travellers only. The local people attended the inn only when a public show was offered. For daily purposes they had their own establishments, the taverns, and there were strict laws against townspeople "tippling in inns," which existed only for the receipt and refreshment of travellers.

The gaming-houses and the houses of assignation seem to have operated then much as they do now. The better kind of gaming-house was, like the better kind to-day, an elegantly furnished private house. It gave, as in Mayfair to-day, a free and lavish supper on the host—fish, fowl, pasties, jellies, marchpane cakes, with abundance of wines. The visitor was as free to enjoy these things when he won as when he lost. The games chiefly played were Hazard, Primero, Gleek, Post and Pair, Ruff, and Tick-Tack; and play went on all night. The other houses were also conducted in a manner of which the tradition survives to-day. They were, like ours, luxuriously arranged and decorated, and they too offered free refreshment—though refreshment of a special kind with a view to its effect—as stewed prunes, a term frequently used as an allusion to such places; oyster-pies; muscadine; raw eggs; wine with a sprig of bugloss.

Under the Tudors the midnight masques and revels became even more elaborate. Cavendish, in his *Life of Wolsey*, gives a description of some of the entertainments prepared by the Cardinal at Hampton Court, for his King:

The banquets were set forth, with masks and mummeries, in so gorgeous a sort, and costly manner, that it was a heaven to behold. There wanted no dames or damsels meet or apt to dance with the maskers or to garnish the place for the time, with other goodly disports. Then was there all kind of music and harmony set forth, with excellent voices both of men and children. I have seen the King suddenly come in thither in a mask, with a dozen of other maskers, all in garments like shepherds, made of fine cloth of gold and fine crimson satin paned, and caps of the same, with visors of good proportion of visnomy; their hairs and beards either of fine gold wire, or else of silver, and some being of black silk; having sixteen torch-bearers, besides their drums, and other persons attending upon them, with visors, and clothed all in satin of the same colours.

A Sixteenth-century Gaming-house

He describes a mock-surprise which Henry, with the connivance of Wolsey, worked on the company at one of Wolsey's dinners. Shakespeare made use of it in Act I of *King Henry VIII*. The dinner was, for a Wolsey dinner, a small and intimate affair—only about two hundred guests—and the teeming procession of dishes was being heartily enjoyed, when the company was startled by a salute of guns. Wolsey, pretending ignorance, sent his Lord Chamberlain to see what was happening, and the Lord Chamberlain brought news that some nobleman had arrived in the river with a retinue, as it might be some ambassador from a foreign prince. Wolsey then desired him to receive the visitors and invite them to join the banquet and share in the pastime. They were then brought in with an escort of twenty torches and drums and fifes, and marched towards Wolsey in his chair of state and gravely saluted him. The visitors then produced a cup of gold coins, and engaged with the company in various dicing games, sometimes winning and sometimes losing. When these games were done, they took the cup of coins to Wolsey, and offered him one cast for the whole. He threw a winning cast.

Then, Cavendish goes on, he asked the visitors if there was not among them some noble man who would be more worthy than himself to occupy the chair of state and to whom, if they would make him known, he would gladly resign it. They answered that there was among them one superior to the others, and if Wolsey could distinguish him he would accept the seat of honour. Wolsey, searching among them, picked out one with a black beard who, in his make-up, had some resemblance to the King, but was a member of the court, Sir Edward Neville. Whereupon the King, until then unnoticed, pulled down his visor and that of Sir Edward, and disclosed himself, on which the company, finding that the King was among them, "rejoiced very much."

The King then changed his clothes in an ante-chamber and reappeared in new and princely garments:

> And in the time of the King's absence the dishes of the banquet were clean taken up, and the tables spread again with new and sweet perfumed cloths; every man sitting still until the King and his maskers came in among them again, every man being newly apparelled. Then the King took his seat under the cloth of state, commanding no man to remove, but sit still, as they did before. Then in came a new banquet before the king's majesty, and to all the rest through the tables, wherein, I suppose, were served two hundred dishes or above, of wondrous costly meats and devices, subtilly devised. Thus passed forth the whole night with banqueting, dancing, and other triumphant devices, to the great comfort of the King and pleasant regard of the nobility there assembled.

There was then no public amusement at night: no public play, dance, concert, assembly, or illuminated garden. Those things came later, and, as repressive authority might have foreseen, when they came they brought a civilising influence; the gaming and other night houses were less frequented. But sometimes the ordinary outside people were admitted to the halls of the great houses as spectators of the masques and balls, and on special occasions, such as wedding celebrations, the feast, as well as the entertainment, was open to all comers in their respective rank, above or below the salt. This custom was followed in London by the Mayor, if Hentzner, who was sometimes wrong, may be trusted. The Mayor, he says, during the year of his magistracy, "is obliged to live so magnificently that foreigner or native, without any expense, is free, if he can find a chair empty, to dine at his table, where there is always the greatest plenty."

When, under Elizabeth, the first theatres arrived, growing out of the open-air Mysteries and Moralities and the performances of Interludes in inn-yards, they were, like ours of to-day, afternoon affairs. The abnormal social conditions of 1941 are akin to the normal social conditions of that time, and have brought us in many matters to order our

A Sixteenth-century Concert

lives as though we were Elizabethans. Since their streets at night were as dark and as dangerous, in another way, as our town streets, the theatre could not give night performances. The hour then was three o'clock, and it continued to be the hour until the end of the seventeenth century when better lighting made night performances possible. The only dramatic performances at night were those given privately in the Halls of the Universities or the Inns of Court. The evening under Elizabeth and the first two Stuarts offered, as before, only the tavern; though the law against night tippling seems to have operated rather for the benefit of the constables than against the tipplers:

> The pillage of the night is only mine, mine own fee simple.... Now we'll go search the taverns, commit such as we find drinking, and be drunk ourselves with what we take from them. These silly wretches whom I for form's sake only have brought hither shall watch without and guard us.

An odd pastime for vigorous youth forbidden any other decent outlet at night was concerned with campanology. Hentzner speaks of the

5 A Torchlight Procession in the Sixteenth Century

6 An Elizabethan "Stag Party"

7 Bringing in the Yule Log in the Great Hall at Penshurst, Kent
A Tudor reconstruction by Joseph Nash

English love of noise, "such as the firing of cannons, drums, and the ringing of bells, so that it is common for a number of them that have got a glass in their heads to go up into some belfry, and ring the bells for hours together for the sake of exercise." Sometimes teams of ringers challenged other teams, as they do in country districts in our own times, when ringing is allowed. This night pastime, which apparently gave no consideration to those who wanted to sleep, was called A Match to Ring.

A pastime at private parties was the Lottery. Just as some vulgar rich of later times have given dinner-parties with a £100 bank-note in each napkin, so the wealthy of those days would buy popularity by making a ceremonial lottery of their pictures or jewels with tickets at nominal prices. Chapman, in one of his comedies, has a scene turning on this custom:

> I come to you from my master, who would pray you speak to Lemot, that Lemot might speak to the King that my master's lottery for his jewels may go forward. He hath made the rarest device that ever you heard. We have Fortune in it, and she our maid plays, and I and my fellow carry two torches, and our boy goes before and speaks a speech.

The custom is not quite dead. I recall a book-auction in New York which was conducted on somewhat the same lines. One book was to be put up—a First Folio or a Caxton or something of that sort. The principal dealers and collectors were invited to a dinner. At one end of the dining-room was a curtained dais. When the excellent dinner was done, all the lights were lowered, the curtains of the dais were drawn, and there, under a spotlight, was a fair maid robed in white, standing at a lectern and turning over the leaves of the precious volume. This scene was "held" for something over a minute, while the maid read a paragraph or so from the work. Then up went the lights and the auctioneer snapped into business.

Another play of Chapman's, *The Ball*, mentions another mode of party-giving that survives to-day. It is that by which people who have no town house contrive to give the impression that they have, by hiring a furnished Mayfair house for a dinner and dance; while those who do possess a Mayfair house are not above making a bit out of it in this way, like any seaside landlady. In Chapman's play, the dancing-master, supervising arrangements, complains that "My lord hire dis house of the city merchant. It smell musty." Shakespeare's plays afford many sidelights on those private revels and other night festivities. The alleged period of the play may be fifteenth or fourteenth century, and the place may be Venice or Denmark or Illyria or Padua or Athens, but the manners and customs and speech are always those of the England of his own time. The supper-party at the Boar's Head in the second part of *Henry IV*, the supper and masked-ball at the mansion of the Capulets, and the midnight racket of Sir Toby Belch and Sir Andrew are such affairs as Shakespeare himself must have witnessed. The Sir Toby Belch scene, indeed, might have reproduced that legendary drinking-party of which Shakespeare is supposed to have made one,

A Bachelor Party in the Seventeenth Century

when the tipplers of Stratford challenged the topers of Bidford. The Stratford men were so defeated that they could not get home, and spent the night under a hedge. A fit of penitence produced the well-known jingle about drinking with:

> Piping Pebworth, Dancing Marston,
> Haunted Hillborough, Hungry Grafton,
> Dodging Exhall, Papist Wixford,
> Beggarly Broom and Drunken Bidford.

In *Twelfth Night* Sir Toby Belch and Sir Andrew Aguecheek are discovered by the Clown in a room in Olivia's house, and the talk is thoroughly English:

Sir Toby. Approach, Sir Andrew: not to be abed after midnight is to be up betimes; and *diluculo surgere*, thou know'st—

Sir And. Nay, by my troth, I know not; but I know to be up late is to be up late.

Sir Toby. A false conclusion: I hate it as an unfilled can. To be up after midnight and to go to bed then, is early; so that to go to bed after midnight is to go to bed betimes. Does not our life consist of the four elements?

Sir And. Faith, so they say; but I think it rather consists of eating and drinking.

Sir Toby. Thou art a scholar; let us therefore eat and drink. Marian, I say! a stoup of wine!

(*Enter* CLOWN)

Sir And. Here comes the fool, i'faith.
Clown. How now, my hearts! did you never see the picture of 'we three'?
Sir Toby. Welcome, ass. Now let's have a catch. ...

"A Brown Dozen of Drunkards" (1648)

Sir And. A mellifluous voice, as I am true knight.
Sir Toby. A contagious breath.
Sir And. Very sweet and contagious, i'faith.
Sir Toby. To hear by the nose, it is dulcet in contagion. But shall we make the welkin dance indeed? Shall we rouse the night-owl in a catch that will draw three souls out of one weaver? shall we do that?
Sir And. An you love me, let's do't; I am dog at a catch. ...

(*Enter* MARIA)

Mar. What a caterwauling do you keep here! If my lady have not called up her steward Malvolio and bid him turn you out of doors, never trust me.
Sir Toby. My lady's a Cataian, we are politicians, Malvolio's a Peg-a-Ramsey, and *Three merry men we be.* Am not I consanguineous? am I not of her blood? Tillyvally, Lady! *There dwelt a man in Babylon, lady, lady!*
Clown. Beshrew me, the knight's in admirable fooling.
Sir And. Ay, he does well enough if he be disposed, and so do I too; he does it with a better grace, but I do it more natural.
Sir Toby. O, *the twelfth day of December*——
Mar. For the love o' God, peace!

(*Enter* MALVOLIO)

Mal. My masters, are you mad? or what are you? Have you no wit, manners, nor honesty, but to gabble like tinkers at this time of night? Do ye make an alehouse of my lady's house, that ye squeak out your coziers' catches without any mitigation or remorse of voice? Is there no respect of place, persons, nor time in you?

Sir Toby. We did keep time, sir, in our catches. Sneck up!

Mal. Sir Toby, I must be round with you. My lady bade me tell you that though she harbours you as her kinsman, she's nothing allied to your disorders. If you can separate yourself and your misdemeanours, you are welcome to the house; if not, an it would please you to take leave of her, she is very willing to bid you farewell.

Sir Toby. Farewell, dear heart, since I must needs be gone.
Mar. Nay, good Sir Toby.
Clown. His eyes do show his days are almost done.
Mal. Is't even so?
Sir Toby. But I will never die.
Clown. Sir Toby, there you lie.
Mal. This is much credit to you.
Sir Toby. Shall I bid him go?
Clown. What an if you go?
Sir Toby. Shall I bid him go and spare not?
Clown. O no, no, no, no, you dare not.
Sir Toby. 'Out o' tune!' Sir, ye lie. Art any more than a steward? Dost thou think, because thou art virtuous, there shall be no more cakes and ale?
Clown. Yes, by Saint Anne, and ginger shall be hot i' the mouth.

An evening diversion at private parties in Elizabethan times was one that has a touch of the Victorian *Evenings At Home*, though since the women of the sixteenth century were more widely educated than those of the middle nineteenth, the affairs no doubt had some fire and salt. This particular diversion was the mixed debate or dispute on given topics. There is a scene in Lyly's *Euphues and his England*, in which the company, after supper, consider how to pass the night. The Lady Flavia addresses them:

Gentlemen and Gentlewomen, these Lenten evenings be long, and a shame it were to go to bed; cold they are, and therefore folly it were to walk abroad; to play at Cards is common, at Chess tedious, at Dice unseemly, with Christmas games, untimely. In my opinion therefore, to pass away these long nights, I would have some pastime that might be pleasant, but not unprofitable, rare, but not without reasoning; so shall we all account the Evening well spent, be it never so long, which otherwise would be tedious, were it never so short.

The company consists of the ladies Flavia, Camilla, and Frances, and the men are Surius, Philautus, Martius, and Euphues. Surius, the chief of the men, agrees with Flavia in the matter of sensible pastime, and the company leave the choice with her. She chooses the Debate:

"Your task, Surius, shall be to dispute with Camilla, and choose your own argument, Philautus shall argue with mistress Frances, Martius with my self. And all having finished their discourses, Euphues shall be as judge, who hath done best, and whatsoever he shall allot either for reward, to the worthiest, or for penance to the worst, shall be presently accomplished." This liked them all exceedingly.

Elizabeth herself is said to have filled her evenings with the company of men of wit and learning, and to have taken a leading part in their discussions, and not only by virtue of her queenship. Those evenings should have been salty enough, even if they did not go so far as Mark Twain's conjectured account of them as presented in his ribald and privately printed *Fireside Conversation, 1601*. They would at least, one imagines, be as spirited as those contests at the Mermaid, celebrated by Beaumont and by Fuller; perhaps richer in matter, since the lady in the Chair would have prevented any eccentric wandering from the subject under discussion.

But the favourite night entertainment was still the masque, and it continued to be the favourite under James I and Charles I. At their courts, while it became even more elaborate as a spectacle, exceeding anything to be seen at the theatres, it became also more serious in dramatic substance and in performance. Thomas Heywood and Jonson (and later Shirley) did some of their best work in the masque form, and gave it poetic quality; Inigo Jones designed the settings, and even Bacon condescended in an offhand tone to devote one of the Essays to "these trifles":

> Let the scenes abound with light specially coloured and varied: And let the masquers or any others that are to come down from the scene have some Motions upon the scene itself before their coming down: For it draws the eye strangely and makes it with great pleasure to desire to see that it cannot perfectly discern. Let the songs be loud and cheerful, and not chirpings or pulings. Let the music likewise be sharp and loud and well placed. The colours that show best by candle-light are—White, Carnation, and a kind of sea-water-green, and Oes or Spangs, as they are of no great cost, so they are of most glory. As for rich embroidery it is lost and not discerned. Let the suits of the masquers be graceful and such as become the person when the vizars are off—not after examples of known attires: Turks, Soldiers, Marines, and the like. Let the Anti-Masques not be long: They have been commonly of Fools, Satyrs, Baboons, Wild Men, Antiques, Beasts, Spirits, Witches, Ethiopes, Pigmies, Turquets, Nymphs, Rustics, Cupids and the like. But chiefly let the music of them be recreative and with some strange changes. Some sweet odours suddenly coming forth without any drops falling are, in such a company, as there is steam and heat, things of great pleasure and refreshment.

The last suggestion links us once again with those times. It was only a few years ago that some modern composer, one of *Les Six*, perhaps, who are now numbered with the other half-dozen, proposed to have his symphony performed to the accompaniment of varied perfumes; thinking in his optimism that this would help his audience to understand what he was getting at.

There was one occasion, at the court of James I, when, owing to Royal hospitality, the performance of a midnight masque was not up to the common standard which had then been reached. The occasion was that unfortunate State visit of the King of Denmark, which became a prolonged carousal, and the place was Theobalds, at Cheshunt. Leigh Hunt quotes a letter of Sir John Harrington included in the *Secret History of the Court of James I*:

> I think the Dane hath strangely wrought on our good English nobles; for those whom I could never get to taste good liquor, now follow the fashion, and wallow in beastly delights. The ladies abandon their sobriety, and are seen to roll about in intoxication. . . .

The masque was a representation of Solomon's temple and the coming of the Queen of Sheba with precious gifts for the Scotch Solomon and his brother-in-law. She was to be followed by Hope, Faith, and Charity, who would confer their qualities upon the two kings; by Victory, who would hand them her sword; and then by Peace who would pronounce a benediction. It fell out like this:

> The lady who did play the Queen's part . . . forgetting the steps arising to the canopy, overset her caskets into his Danish Majesty's lap, and fell at his feet, though I think it was rather in his face. Much was the hurry and confusion; cloths and napkins were at hand to make all clean. His Majesty then got up and would dance with the Queen of Sheba; but he fell down and humbled himself before her, and was carried to an inner chamber, and laid on a bed of state, which was not a little defiled with the presents of the Queen which had been bestowed on his garments; such as wine, cream, jelly, beverage, cakes, spices, and other good matters. The entertainment and show went forward, and most of the presenters went backward or fell down; wine did so occupy their upper chambers. . . . Hope did essay to speak, but wine rendered her endeavours so feeble that she withdrew, and hoped the King would excuse her brevity. Faith was then all alone, for I am certain she was not joined to good works, and left the court in a staggering condition. Charity came to the King's feet, and seemed to cover the multitude of sins her sisters had committed; in some sort she made obeyance. . . . Next came Victory, in bright armour, and presented a rich sword to the King, who did not accept it, but put it by with his hand; and by a strange medley of versification did endeavour to make suit to the King. But Victory did not triumph long; for, after much lamentable utterance, she was led away like a silly captive, and laid to sleep on the outer steps of the ante-chamber. Now did Peace make entry, and

strive to get foremost to the King; but I grieve to tell how great wrath she did discover unto those of her attendants. ...

The marriage of the princess Elizabeth, daughter of James, was also celebrated by a masque—this time properly presented. It was done, says Howes in his *Annals*, at the Banqueting House in Whitehall, by lords and ladies, with many delicate devices and much melodious music. It was in three parts: a rustic masque, the usual anti-masque, and the main masque. The last was a masque of knights wearing doublets of carnation satin (the colour recommended by Bacon) decked with stars of silver plate, with spangles of silver lace, Venetian hose and silk carnation stockings, with garters and roses according to their orders. The chief masquers arrived at the Banqueting House by water in the King's barge, "plenteously furnished with a great number of war-lights," and the minor performers followed in galleys, each galley carrying a flare of torches, making "so rare and brave a show upon the water as the like was never seen upon the Thames."

Fireworks as an evening entertainment had been introduced some years earlier, but they were not widely used; they were considered dangerous. That they *were* dangerous is shown by the disaster which happened at the inauguration of a Mayor of Norwich in 1611. By way of thanks to the citizens for his election he decided to give them a night's amusement with a firework display. During the display something went wrong; the fireworks became a fire; and over one hundred and fifty people lost their lives. Nobody, it seems, was responsible; the disaster was attributed to "the will of God." It is curious that such a disaster should have happened on the first day of the mayoralty of a man whose surname was—Anguish.

The night amusements of the ordinary townspeople remained as they were in the fifteenth century. Dekker, writing of London nights in his *Seven Deadly Sinnes*, attributes all sorts of evils to the hours of candle-light; but his accounts, like those of most of his fellow-pamphleteers, must be taken as somewhat enlarged from the actual. They make good reading, as they were meant to do, but as serious indictments they carry little more weight than their modern equivalents, those "exposures" of the underworld made by our more slapdash Sunday papers. They presented anyway the doings of only a small section; but even if the loose behaviour had been general, the spectacle of such infirm characters as Dekker, Greene, Nashe, and Chettle raising lamentations about it presents a perfect case of Satan reproving sin.

With the coming of candle-light, says our author (writing in the first years of the seventeenth century) the shops begin to shut up, and all the city looks like a private play-house as if some dismal tragedy were about to be acted. The damask-coated citizen, having sat all day in his shop, waits for candle-light-time to sneak out and slip into a tavern. The younger shop-keepers, even those lately married, slip off to one of the night-houses for drinking, dancing, and dicing, while the young wife is left at home in solitude, which she is apt to break by inviting in some handsome young friend. The sober Puritan creeps out to the

A Seventeenth-century Tavern Scene

suburbs of Bankside or Smithfield, and enters some stewed-prune house. The kitchen-maids of the big houses invite their friends to private feasts at the cost of their masters. The 'prentices make love to their masters' daughters, with a candle set on the landing so that nobody can come upon them without being seen in advance. The bankrupts, who cannot go out by day for fear of arrest, walk out boldly at nightfall, and "step into some privileged tavern, and there drink healths and pay both drawers and fiddlers after midnight with other men's money, and then march home again fearless of the blows that any shoulder-clapper durst give them." Servants steal out with parcels of their employers' goods, and clerks rifle the till for money to carry to their favourite madam. All this is presented as a catalogue of night-life "villainies." But if Dekker's muck-rake could bring in nothing blacker, one feels that he must have assumed a strong colouring of the Puritan mind to have found in those follies his Seven Deadly Sinnes.

Under James I the taverns (i.e. restaurants and ordinaries, as distinct from ale-houses) could keep open till a fairly late hour, and often were open all night. The Mitre, in Wood Street; the Mermaid, in Bread Street; the Three Cranes, in Thames Street; the Falcon, on Bankside; the German restaurants in the Steelyard at Dowgate Hill; the Boar's Head, Eastcheap; and the Devil tavern, near Temple Bar, were the scenes of many late suppers recorded in the literature of the time. Ben Jonson used both the Mitre and his own Apollo Club, held at the Devil tavern, in more than one of his plays. Other dramatists used the Apollo Room, sometimes approvingly, sometimes satirically. In it Jonson gathered around him the younger poets and poetasters to whom he was pleased to be Father. They were mostly of the minor degree—Marmion, Thomas Randolph, James Howell, Lucius Cary, Cleveland; the one true poet who was proud to be a Son of Ben was Herrick.

The rules of behaviour which he drew up in Latin for members of the Apollo, the *Leges Conviviales*, were painted on a board and hung above the fireplace. The board still exists as the property of the bank built on the site of the old tavern. A versified, and rather jog-trot, translation was made of the twenty-four laws, and one or two of the verses give an idea of the whole:

> As the fund of our pleasure let each pay his shot,
> Except some chance friend whom a member brings in.
> Far hence be the sad, the lewd fop, and the sot,
> For such have the plagues of good company been.
>
> Let the learned and witty, the jovial and gay,
> The generous and honest compose our free state;
> And the more to exalt our delight while we stay,
> Let none be debarred from his choice female mate. . . .
>
> Let the contests be rather of books than of wine.
> Let the company be neither noisy nor mute.
> Let none of things serious, much less divine,
> When belly and Head's full, profanely dispute.
>
> Let no saucy fiddler presume to intrude,
> Unless he is sent for to vary our bliss.
> With mirth, wit, and dancing and singing conclude
> To regale every sense, with delight in excess. . . .
>
> Whoever shall publish what's said, or what's done,
> Be he banished for ever our assembly divine.
> Let the freedom we take be perverted by none,
> To make any guilty by drinking good wine.

His play, *The Staple of News*, has a supper-scene in the Apollo Room, with women guests and the usual entertainment after supper of fiddlers and a singing boy. The main theme of this play shows how yet another of our modern customs was anticipated. We have with us to-day a number of young men who earn a living by gossip-grubbing—advertising smart restaurants and the smart nobodies who use them with silly paragraphs about having seen Lord This or That at So-and-so's. The idea was even then in the air.

The Staple of News was to be a news-agency, with scouts to collect rare and startling intelligence from all parts of London. When some of the characters are talking of the company at the Apollo Room, one of them, Shunwell, turns to the gossip-scouts with: "Sirs, you must get of this news, to store your office—who dines and sups in the town; where and with whom; it will be beneficial; when you are stored, and as we like our fare, we shall reward you." The remark of another character comes even closer to our own time. When one remembers the salaries paid to our modern gossip-grubbers, there is a very up-to-date ring about the character's reference to the gossip-service as "A mighty thing; they talk six thousand a year."

That dining-out and supping-out in taverns, by women as well as men, was beginning to be fashionable is shown by the talk in Shirley's *Lady of Pleasure*:

> *Bornwell*. I have invited a covey of ladies, and as many gentlemen, to-morrow, to the Italian Ordinary; I shall have rarities and regalias to pay for, madam; music, wanton songs, and tunes of silken petticoats to dance to.
> *Lady B*. And to-morrow I have invited half the court to dine here. . . . After dinner I entertain them with a play.
> *Born*. By that time your play inclines to the epilogue, shall we quit our Italian host, and whirl in coaches to the Dutch magazine of sauce, the Stillyard, where deal and backrag, and what strange wine else they dare but give a name to in the reckoning, shall flow into our room, and drown Westphalias, tongues, and anchovies, like some little town endangered by a sluice. . . .

Domestic evening amusements in vogue at the time include some that are in use to-day—cards, dice, tables, shovel-board, chess, the philosophers' game (I can't discover what that was) small-trunks, shuttlecock, billiards, frolicks, purposes, questions-and-commands, etc. These are named by Robert Burton as possible alleviations of the Melancholy which he anatomised. The chief midnight amusement of the madder spirits and roaring boys was one that began when authority first set its control on the life of the dark hours, and thus invited reprisals from the irreverent—that is, everybody except the lymphatic. The game was Beating the Watch. Plays and pamphlets of the period make frequent reference to that sport, and one of the characters in Heywood's *Wise Woman of Hogsdon* (Hoxton) uses it to serve him in an emergency:

"Nay, but hear me, sweet Sir Harry. Being somewhat late at supper at the Mitre, the doors were shut at my lodging; I knocked at three or four places more; all were a-bed, and fast; inns, taverns, none would give me entertainment. Now, would you have had me despaired, and lain in the streets? No, I bethought me of a trick worth two of that, and presently devised, having at that time a charge of money about me, to be lodged, and safely too."

"As how, I pray you?"

"Marry, thus: I had knocked my heels against the ground a good while, knew not where to have a bed for love or money. Now what did I, but, spying the watch, went and hit the constable a good souse on the ear, who provided me of a lodging presently."

Even as late as forty years ago the Strand and Leicester Square, and some of our University towns, were familiar with the night amusement of "knocking policemen about." It was an amusement which ceased only when amusements grew in number and became more varied and more decorous.

The cock-pit was a favourite diversion among all classes. Pepys records a visit to one newly set up in Shoe Lane, and notes the varied company, from Parliament-men to bakers, brewers, butchers, draymen, and what-not. It was a scene that can be matched on any race-course of to-day, and his comment must have occurred to many people seeing a race-meeting for the first time—how strange it was to see people who looked as if they had not bread to put into their mouths laying out three or four pounds on each event, and losing it with no more than a shrug. But under the Stuarts gaming was general. It was recognised and officially permitted, and a regular evening pastime was a visit to the gaming-tables at the Groom-Porter's apartment.

The Groom-Porter was a Court official whose duties were concerned with seeing to the furniture of the Royal rooms, setting the right number of chairs for state occasions, and so on. The gaming-tables which he was permitted to keep were a perquisite of his office, and the grant of them gave him and such deputies as he chose to appoint full power to "supervise, regulate, and authorise all manner of gaming within the kingdom." After the Restoration, gaming was recklessly pursued in Court circles. Pepys was no friend to it, but he did once or twice look in at the Groom-Porter's: "and to see the formality of the groome-porter, who is their judge of all disputes in play and all quarrels that may arise therein, and how his under-officers are there to observe true play at each table, and to give new dice, is a consideration I never could have thought had been in the world." Play began at eight o'clock, and got fully into swing around midnight, when the big plungers came on.

Grammont was one of the plungers, and a lucky one, as his senior, St. Evremond, pointed out: "You play from morning to night, or to speak more properly from night to morning, without knowing what it is to lose. Far from losing the money you brought hither, as you have done in other places, you have doubled it, trebled it, multiplied it almost beyond your wishes. . . ."

The games in Stuart times, in addition to those mentioned earlier (such as Primo, Gleek, and Hazard) were Novum, Flam, Mumchance, One-and-Thirty, New Cut and My Sow's Pigg'd. Every Twelfth Night it was a custom for the play to be led by the King, who usually came off a winner, but stopped whenever the Royal purse had lost £100. This annual setting of bad example to the subjects of the realm often aroused criticism, but it persisted through Queen Anne up to the time of the third George, when the office of Groom-Porter was abolished.

Another Twelfth Night diversion popular with the Stuarts were the Revels of the Inner and Middle Temple. Often these were silly, ill-arranged affairs, but one of them, specially devised by James Shirley, was on an elaborate scale. It was done at midnight at the Banqueting House, with scenes designed by Inigo Jones. The company assembled in their costimes and head-dresses at Ely House, Holborn, and proceeded by Chancery Lane and the Strand to Whitehall, some in chariots, others on foot bearing scores of torch-lights. When the revels were ended, somewhere in the middle of the night, those who had taken part were entertained by the King to a sumptuous supper. Allowing for the difference in money value, that one-night affair cost as much as the production of one of our long-running, equally over-done musical plays. The sum spent on it, £21,000, would be, in money of our own time, about £50,000. Evelyn regarded these shows with contempt: "an old but riotous custome, and has relation neither to virtue nor policy." Elsewhere he calls it "the solemn foolery."

For the evenings of summer, most towns had a bowling-green which was used not only for the game of bowls but as a place of general resort. Grammont, reported by Anthony Hamilton, speaks of the game as being in France the pastime of mechanics and servants only, while in England it is "the exercise of gentlemen, and requires both art and address." The bowling-greens he describes as "little square grass-plots where the turf is almost as smooth and level as the cloth of a billiard-table. As soon as the heat of the day is over, all the company assemble there; they play deep, and spectators are at liberty to make what bets they please." He speaks of the bowling-green at Tunbridge Wells (to which Charles and his Court once went for the waters) as the place of general evening assembly for the courtiers and the harem which always accompanied Charles; "where, in the open air, those who choose dance upon a turf more soft and smooth than the finest carpet in the world." Bowls is a placid pastime, but a modern Skip would, I imagine, lose all his placidity if he caught the village lads and lasses turning the turf of his green into a dance-floor.

Towns with a river used it on light evenings as they do to-day for boating, sailing, and other diversions. But they did it in a modest way; not in the lavish style of Charles and his friends. In our own times we have witnessed at our hotels the displays of millionaires, their "freak" dinners for which they turn courtyards into lagoons or Polar ice-fields, and dress waiters as gondoliers or Eskimos. But the nobility of the past were not much more advanced in the true civilisation of the middle way than our *nouveaux riches*, and Grammont, from the country which has always been credited with taste and civilisation, showed little of either when he took a hand in the river-pageants arranged for Charles on evenings when the Park was too hot and dusty. Charles would take the Royal barge at the stairs of Whitehall Palace, and be pulled up and down the river, followed by a train of open boats filled with the court beauties. During the progress he would be served with a profuse collation, and entertained with music and fireworks:

> The Chevalier de Grammont always made one of the company, and it was very seldom that he did not add something of his own invention, agreeably to surprise by some unexpected stroke of magnificence and gallantry. Sometimes he had complete concerts of vocal and instrumental music, which he privately brought from Paris, and which struck up on a sudden in the midst of these parties; sometimes he gave banquets, which likewise came from France, and which, even in the midst of London, surpassed the King's collations. These entertainments sometimes exceded, at others fell short of his expectations, but they always cost him an immense deal of money.

The term *décadent* was not to be in particular use till over two hundred years later, but the court of the second Charles, in its efforts to beguile his saturnine Majesty, seems to have known that state expressed in the later cry for madder music and for stronger wine. There is a story of an evening at Bristol, when the court was at its silliest, and search was made for some new stupidity to relieve the tedium of living. Frances Stewart, one of the leading favourites, was being entertained by some old lord with his latest trick; he was teaching her how to hold a lighted candle in her mouth without blowing it out. Another courtier, boasting a large mouth, and hoping to make favour with the Stewart, thereupon took two lighted candles into his mouth, and walked three times round the room with them, keeping them burning all the way, and reducing the Stewart to hysterics.

More sensible evening diversions were those of the glee and madrigal groups which appeared about this time, in London and elsewhere, meeting at taverns or at the house of one of the members, for social singing-parties. Pepys often had singing-parties with his friends and servants, at home or on the water, and once or twice attended the Music Meetings held at the General Post Office in Bishopsgate. About 1670 there was a Music Society with rooms in Old Jewry, which published a song-book of catches and glees for parties of this kind—*The Catch-that-Catch Can, or the Metrical Companion*; and in 1678 Thomas Britton, the Musical Small-Coal Man, started his concerts in the loft above his coal-store, and drew all London. His place was at Jerusalem Passage, Clerkenwell, and in that small room in that obscure byway he gave every Thursday night for forty years the best music to be heard anywhere in London. At some of the later concerts Handel and Pepuschi played. His loft was filled with rank and fashion; every distinguished foreigner who came to London was treated to one of Thomas Britton's concerts; and all the time he continued to hawk his coal about the streets, and to be, to all appearance, nothing but a coal-man. Yet scholars, famous musicians and dilettanti were glad to sit with him and enjoy the taste and learning displayed in his talk. Matthew Prior, in an elegy upon him, speaks of him as "so bright a genius in so dark a sphere":

> Though doom'd to small coal, yet to arts allied;
> Rich without wealth, and famous without pride,
> Music's best patron, judge of books and men;
> Belov'd and honour'd by Apollo's train.

He was no miser, hawking coal in order to increase his money. It was his living, and the money it brought was expended in musical instruments, books of general literature, books on chemistry and the occult, and in those free concerts. It was his interest in the occult that was largely responsible for his death. Some practical joker, knowing his belief in the world of spirits, thought to amuse the company at one of the Thursday gatherings by giving him a fright. The fool brought along a ventriloquist who threw a voice from nowhere telling Britton that his time was short, and exhorting him to fall on his knees and prepare to meet his God. Accepting this as a genuine phenomenon, Britton did as the voice commanded, and then took to his bed, and two days later died.

About the middle of the seventeenth century the coffee-house had

come in, and was spreading a new fashion in evening rendezvous. The
first place of the kind established in London was Pasqua Rosee's, off
Cornhill. The success of this soon brought companions to it, and in
quick succession came Farr's, the Jerusalem, the Jamaica, Garraway's
and Jonathan's (both in Change Alley), and Dick's, by Temple Bar.
By the end of the century the town was thick with them. John Ashton,
in one of his social histories, gives a list of London coffee-houses at the
beginning of the next century. They number four-hundred-and-eighty,
and include one or two names that are familiar to men of to-day—such
as Anderton's, Fleet Street, the Bay Tree, St. Swithin's Lane, and the
Rainbow, Temple Bar. Other famous houses were the wits' and poets'
houses—Will's, Tom's and Button's, in Russell Street; the Smyrna, Pall
Mall; the St. James, in St. James' Street; Slaughter's, St. Martin's Lane;
the Bedford, Covent Garden; Turk's Head, Gerrard Street; Child's,
St. Paul's Churchyard; the Grecian, Devereux Court; White's, St.
James' Street; and the Piazza, Covent Garden.

To the man about town of those days, who usually lived in lodgings
up three or four pairs of stairs, they were a boon. He paid a penny at
the bar for admission (a sort of *couvert* charge for lights, fire, journals,
etc.) and could then take his seat in a box, call for whatever he could
pay for, read the papers, or move about the room and listen to the
general talk, and join it. He could have his letters addressed there; he
could make appointments with his business or social acquaintances, and
leave word with the girl at the bar as to where he was to be found at
such and such an hour; he could use the servants of the place to carry
messages or run errands. He could make it, indeed, his home for most
of the day and all the night; the place where he was to be seen or
"heard of."

More expensive night diversion was to be had in the old Spring
Garden, by Whitehall and the new Garden at Vauxhall. Those places
were frequented until midnight, and light suppers could be had there,
though Vauxhall, of course, was not then what it became in the next
century. There was no entertainment; only gravelled walks and arbours
and a nightingale or so; and the refreshments were little more than
jellies, syllabubs, and tarts.

For the ordinary and poorer people there was still little amusement
after dark. The streets were still badly lighted, and for the majority
the rule was still Early to Bed. Then, towards the end of the century,
the club, or select circle with a subscription and a private room at some
coffee-house (on the lines of the Mermaid and Apollo clubs) developed
into an institution for people of all classes—not only the leisured, but

the merchant, the tradesman, the shopman, and the clerk. They sprang up everywhere, in all large towns, notably the ports and spas and watering-places, and they multiplied as the coffee-houses had done. Club-life, from then onward, was a feature of English night-life, and remained a feature for about two hundred and fifty years—that is, until these present days, when clubs are losing their appeal and their support.

By the time of William III, the introduction of better lighting made other entertainment possible, and the theatre hour which, twenty years earlier, had been three o'clock, was set as late as six o'clock, with dinner at four o'clock. Vanbrugh's Lord Foppington, in *The Relapse*, (1696) describing his daily day, speaks of dining at Locket's Ordinary (by Charing Cross), and then going to the play: "where, till nine o'clock, I entertain myself with looking upon the company; and usually dispose of one hour more in leading them out." With a later hour for the theatre, came later hours for tavern suppers and assemblies, with, of course, later hours for beginning the day. In the next century the fashionable world began to keep still later hours, and seemed to decide that the best of all ways to lengthen their days was to steal a few hours from the night. In this they differed from us of 1941, who have found that for the same object it is better to add a couple of hours to the morning.

8 A Musical Evening in the Reign of Queen Anne
From a painting by Marcellus Laroon

9 A Seventeenth-century Concert

10 "He Revels"

A Plate from 'The Rake's Progress," by William Hogarth

Night into Day

'Tis noise and nonsense are their dear delight
ANON.

BUT THOUGH late hours had become the fashion they were not everywhere popular. The pleasure of turning night into day was not, even in the eighteenth century, everybody's pleasure. Swift, in his *Journal to Stella*, makes frequent complaint of Robert Harley's late hours in town and at Windsor and elsewhere. "He dines too late for my head" . . . "Lord Treasurer kept me till past twelve. . . . He keeps cursed hours." . . . "'Tis now eleven, and a messenger is come from Lord Treasurer to sup with them, but I have excused myself, and am glad I am in bed, for else I should sit up till two." These late sittings led him to compose a verse of self-advice on self-preservation:

> Drink little at a time,
> Put water with your wine,
> Miss your glass when you can,
> And go off the first man.

Pope was another who complained. Spence quotes him as saying of Addison that he "usually studied all the morning, then met his party at Button's, dined there, and stayed five or six hours; and sometimes far into the night. I was of the company for about a year, but found it too much for me; it hurt my health."

Many plays of the time present scenes of complaint between husband and wife on the fashion of late hours. In Farquhar's *Beaux' Stratagem*, the scene of which is the quiet cathedral town of Lichfield, Squire Sullen's wife speaks of her husband: "he came home this morning at his usual hour of four, wakened me out of a sweet dream by tumbling over the tea-table which he broke all to pieces." Vanbrugh's unfinished play, *A Journey to London*, presents a husband-and-wife scene, in which the complainants are reversed:

"But Madam, can you think it a reasonable thing to be abroad till two o'clock in the morning, when you know I go to bed at eleven?"

"And can you think it a wise thing to go to bed at eleven, when you know I am likely to disturb you by coming there at three?"

"Well, the manner of women's living of late is insupportable, and some way or other——"

"It's to be mended, I suppose. Pray, my Lord, one word of fair argument. You complain of my late hours; I of your early ones; so far we are even, you'll allow; but which gives us the best figure in the eye of the polite world? My two o'clock speaks life, activity, spirit, and vigour; your eleven has a dull, drowsy, stupid, good-for-nothing sound with it. It savours much of a mechanick, who must get to bed betimes, that he may rise early to open his shop. Faugh!"

"I thought to go to bed early and rise so, was ever esteemed a right practice for all people."

"Beasts do it. . . . I won't come home till four to-morrow morning."

"I'll order the doors to be locked at twelve."

"Then I won't come home till to-morrow night."

"Then you shall never come home again, madam."

From the first London clubs of the seventeenth century, such as the Apollo, the Rota and the Calves' Head, developed those scores of clubs of the Augustan age, none of which survives to-day. Among them were the October, the Mug-House, the Beefsteak (1709; the first of many of that title), the Society, the Bumper, the Saturday, the Scriblerus, the Kit-Kat, the Golden Fleece, the Sealed Knot, and all sorts of small eccentric clubs which afforded subjects for satirical *Spectator* and *Tatler* essays. None of those clubs had premises of their own in the manner of later days. They met, as I say, at coffee-houses or taverns. One or two met in private houses. These were called Street Clubs, and were formed of the inhabitants of a particular street who wanted evening society but did not care to venture very far at night. Each member took it in turn to open his house and be host once or twice a week, and thus they could find conversation and company within a few paces of their own doors. But those clubs were really no more than a party in a parlour.

John Timbs, in his *Club Life of London*, quotes an account of the nightly proceedings of the first Mug-House Club, which met twice a week during the winter at a house in Long Acre. This first Mug-House was entirely a social affair; it was not until many years later that clubs of this name sprang up all over London and became centres of political faction and sedition, and often of riot. The Long Acre club took its name from one of its customs, whereby the only drink taken was ale, and each member had his particular mug set at his particular place at table. The gathering at the two weekly meetings was usually well over a hundred:

> They have a grave old gentleman, in his own gray hairs, now within a few months of ninety years old, who is their President, and sits in an arm'd chair some steps higher than the rest of the company to keep the whole room in order. A harp plays all the time at the lower end of the room; and every now and then one or other of the company rises and entertains the rest with a song, and some are good masters. . . . The room is always so diverted with songs, and drinking from one table to another to one another's healths, that

there is no room for politics or anything that can sour conversation. One must be there by seven to get room, and after ten the company are for the most part gone.

Ten o'clock seems to have been the usual hour at that time for the breaking-up of club meetings. One of the *Tatler* papers refers to a club of critics which met nightly at the Smyrna Coffee House in Pall Mall, and talked for the benefit of any who cared to listen on music, poetry, and politics between the hours of eight and ten. But the coffee-houses themselves, and the taverns, remained open to a much later hour, and private balls and assemblies went on till the morning. The clubs were much more democratic than those that followed. "Here you will see," a contemporary says, "blue and green ribbons, with stars, sitting familiarly and talking with the same freedom as if they had left their quality and degrees of distance at home; and a stranger tastes with pleasure the universal liberty of speech of the English nation." They had none of the amenities of a club as we know it to-day; nothing more than the tavern or coffee-house could afford; and were only a kind of informal debating society. Some of them, like certain obscure clubs of to-day, took members on the doorstep, on payment of two shillings, and advertised their readiness to do so. Those places were not frequented by the wits. They were mostly started by the landlord for the benefit of his house, and from accounts given of them in the journals of that time they seem to have been pretty dreary affairs; as dreary as their parallels of to-day. The talk was no doubt as piquant as that recorded by Addison's Sober Citizen:

> *Monday.* From Six to Ten. At the Club. Mr. Nisby's opinion about the Peace.
> *Tuesday.* From Six to Ten. At the Club. Mr. Nisby's account of the Great Turk.
> *Wednesday.* Six a clock. Was half an hour in the Club before anybody else came. Mr. Nisby of opinion that the Grand Vizier was not strangled the 6th instant.
> *Friday.* 6 a clock. At the Club as Steward. Sat late.
> *Saturday.* Six. Went to the Club. Like to have faln into a gutter. Grand Vizier certainly dead.

James Puckle's moralising little work, *The Club*, presenting, in a series of "characters," like those of John Earle, Thomas Overbury, and La Bruyère, the members of the Noah's Ark Club, probably gives a fair picture of the types assembled in any of those got-up clubs. Each of them is made to exhibit himself in his folly, and is then dissected for the benefit of ingenuous youth. He shows us a Buffoon, a Gamester, a Critic, a Newsmonger, a Projector, a Quack, a Flatterer, a Rake, a

Travelled Man, a Morose Man, a Wise Man, a Detractor, and so on. In short, a typical club of then or now. In any club variety of character and interest is essential. Thus, in the club presented in the first *Spectator* papers, the members are types of position and occupation, as the Squire, the Lawyer, the Merchant, the army Captain, the Man About Town, and the Parson.

The restaurants of that time, as distinct from coffee-houses, seem to have been well frequented for suppers after the theatre. The leading houses were Pontac's, a French house in Abchurch Lane; the Pope's Head, off Cornhill; Dolly's, between Newgate Street and Paternoster Row; the Salutation and Cat, in Newgate Street; Locket's, at Charing Cross, and the Rummer, a few doors from it; the Mitre, in Fleet Street; the Star and Garter, Pall Mall; the Thatched House, St. James' Street; Chateline's, Covent Garden; the St. Alban's, Pall Mall; the Fountain and the Globe, both in the Strand; and the Devil, already mentioned, which had a life of about two hundred years, its last being 1788. The most expensive of those places were Pontac's and Locket's, where sometimes a single dish for one would figure in the bill at a guinea. The special dishes of the French house were chickens just out of the shell, and ortolans. Regular supper dishes at the other houses about the Queen Anne time were various kinds of game and wildfowl, salmis and fricassés, froises of eggs, fresh-water fish, sucking-pig, and many sorts of pie and pasty.

Gay's description of a meeting of the better sort of club, in his poem on *Wine*, shows that the symposium then was actually a symposium, not the arid mockery invented by modern editors in search of free copy:

> ... when the sun
> Faintly from western skies his rays oblique
> Darts sloping, and to Thetis' wat'ry lap
> Hastens in prone career, with friends select
> Swiftly we hie to Devil Young or Old,
> Jocund and boon, where at the entrance stands
> A stripling, who with scrapes and humil cringe,
> Greets us in winning speech and accent bland.

The company go up to their private room, and when they are seated round the table, the drawer comes for orders:

> Name, sirs, the wine that most invites your taste,
> Champagne or Burgundy or Florence pure,
> Or Hock antique, or Lisbon new or old,
> Bordeaux or neat French White or Alicant.
> For Bordeaux we with voice unanimous
> Declare, such sympathy's in boon compeers.

The wine is served and the Royal toast is drunk, and then:

> A pause ensues, and now with grateful chat
> We improve the interval, and joyous mirth
> Engages our rais'd souls, pat repartee,
> Or witty joke our airy senses moves
> To pleasant laughter, strait the echoing room
> With universal peals and shouts resounds.

They toast Marlborough, and the Ministry, and then each man toasts his mistress of the minute, and then follows desultory talk and discussion; and so the night goes on:

> Thus we the winged hours in harmless mirth
> And joys unsully'd pass, till humid night
> Has half her race perform'd, now all abroad
> Is hush'd and silent, nor the rumbling noise
> Of coach or cart or smoky link-boy's call
> Is heard; but Universal silence reigns;
> When we in merry plight, airy and gay,
> Surprised to find the hours so swiftly fly,
> With hasty knock, or twang of pendant cord,
> Alarm the drowsy youth from slumb'ring nod;
> Startled he flies, and stumbles o'er the stairs
> Erroneous, and with busy knuckles plies
> His yet-clung eyelids, and with stagg'ring reel
> Enters confus'd, and mutt'ring asks our wills:
> When we with liberal hands the score discharge,
> And homeward each his course with steady step
> Unerring steer'd, of cares and coin bereft.

Theatres at that time were few: Drury Lane, the New Theatre in Portugal Street, Lincolns Inn, the Theatre in the Haymarket, and the Opera House, also in the Haymarket. But a lack of theatres did not mean a lack of authors or of new plays. The long run was then unknown, and audiences of those few theatres could see as many new things as audiences of to-day's suburban cinemas. Ten successive nights was considered a good run; five nights meant that the play had succeeded; the rule for most plays was two nights, and possibly a few performances later in the season or in the following season. The play was then the form for most authors; the novel was scarcely known, and had to wait for Richardson to make it a popular form; so plays came out as plentifully as pamphlets. A curious theatre custom of that time gave many hard-up people a chance of seeing the opening of a play—enough to enable them to talk about it in the coffee-houses after it was over, and to give the impression of being up to date in the drama. Money was not taken at the doors. It was collected after the first act, when those who did not wish to stay could go. The modern insult of "walking-out" on a play is thus not new; we do to-day from honest distaste what those hard-up theatre-goers did from necessity posing as distaste.

Another custom was that by which footmen attending their masters and mistresses to the theatre were given free seats in the top gallery. They were often in danger of losing this privilege; they seemed to think that a free seat entitled them to complete freedom in behaviour and comment. The management had often to call them to order, or get their respective masters to turn them out, and periodicals of the time

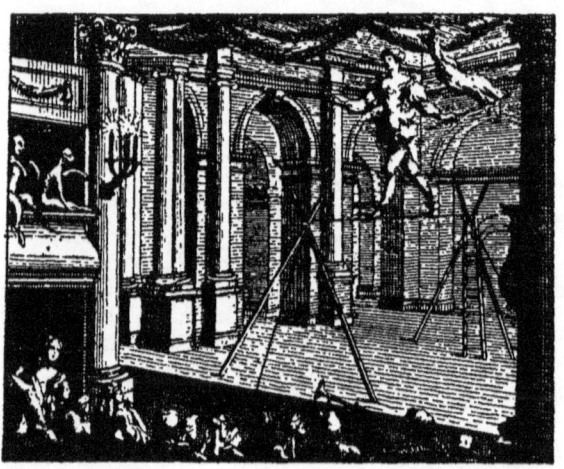

The Interior of a Theatre in the early Eighteenth Century, showing a tightrope act in progress. The occupants of the box are caricatured as monkeys
From a drawing by the architect, William Kent

had many angry paragraphs and verses on their insolence. One of the papers had a dig at them with a supposed advertisement: "Dropt near the Playhouse in the Haymarket, a bundle of horsewhips, designed to belabour the Footmen in the upper gallery, who almost every night this winter have made such an intolerable disturbance that the Players could not be heard."

A description of the interior of the theatre of that time is given by a contemporary:

> The Pit is an amphitheatre, fill'd with benches without backboards, and adorn'd and cover'd with green cloth. Men of quality, particularly the younger sort, some ladies of reputation and virtue, and abundance of damsels

that hunt for prey, sit all together in this place, higgledy-piggledy, chatter, toy, play, hear, hear not. Farther up, against the wall, under the first gallery, and just opposite to the stage, rises another amphitheatre, which is taken up by persons of the best quality, among whom are generally very few men. The galleries, whereof there are only two rows, are filled with none but ordinary people, particularly the upper one.

An essential figure in all theatres was the orange girl. The association of the drama with oranges was long-continued. Even to this day the air of some of our older theatres in the provinces holds a ghostly essence of orange. Those orange wenches did not only sell fruit and other favours; they acted as messengers and go-betweens in cases of the sudden infatuation of a beau with Bright-Eyes in an opposite box. Nicholas Rowe has a verse on those girls and their services:

> See how her charge hangs dangling by the rim,
> See how the balls blush o'er the basket-brim;
> But little those she minds, the cunning belle
> Has other fish to fry, and other fruit to sell;
> See how she whispers yonder youthful peer,
> See how he smiles, and lends a greedy ear.
> At length 'tis done, the note o'er orange wrapt
> Has reached the box, and lays in lady's lap.

The general behaviour of the theatre audience has become quieter since those days. Though sometimes certain women at a modern first-night arouse in the people sitting near them the same irritation felt by Mr. Spectator with the women of his time:

> A little before the rising of the curtain, she broke out into a loud soliloquy, When Will the Dear Witches Enter? and immediately upon their first appearance asked a lady that sat three boxes from her, on her right hand, if those witches were not charming creatures. A little after, as Betterton was in one of the finest speeches of the play, she shook her fan at another lady, who sat as far on the left hand, and told her with a whisper that might be heard all over the pit, We Must Not Expect to See Ballon To-night. Not long after, calling out to a young baronet by his name, who sat three seats before me; she asked him whether Macbeth's wife was still alive; and before he could give an answer, fell a-talking of the ghost of Banquo.

Night-life at the spas and watering-places was not a very late affair. Nash, the social dictator of Bath, when he took office in 1706, ordained that all amusements should end at eleven o'clock. Just as the licensing authorities of our seaside places refuse extended hours to hotels and restaurants, so Nash refused any extension of hours at Bath, whereby invalids might be tempted to indulgences which would undo the good of the treatment they were having. Dinner was usually at four, and after dinner the company drank tea at the Rooms, and at seven o'clock dancing began, and gaming, and raffles. Half-way through the evening came a break for supper (included in the subscription) and then more dancing. But at eleven o'clock, whatever dance might be in progress, and however eager the dancers might be to continue, Nash would appear and stop the music. Even when a Princess once demanded that dancing should continue, and reminded him of her royalty, he reminded her that the laws of the Rooms were his laws, the King of Bath's, and must be observed.

The theatre, or rather the miscellaneous rooms in which travelling companies presented plays, drew little response from either the townspeople or the visitors. Often the "house" all told would be twenty-five people. There was a greater evening pastime than the theatre or even than dancing. The real night-life of Bath was centred on the gaming-tables. Nash himself was a gamester. He received no salary as social director; he lived by dice and cards. Throughout his reign he made the tables the chief attraction of the place, and during the season—a five-months winter season—all the sharpers from London and the Continent travelled down to pluck the young lords and the wealthy citizens. But he did not countenance high play, and the gaming, like the dancing, stopped at eleven. When, some years later, he was invited also to direct affairs at Tunbridge Wells, whose season was summer, he imposed similar laws, and all public life stopped at the same hour.

A writer of the time, who was either Ned Ward or a careful mimic of his style, gives a picture of the Bath evening in which gaming is shown as the main pastime:

> We went to walk in the Grove, a very pleasant place for diversion; there is the Royal Oak and several raffling shops. In one of the walks is several sets of nine-pins and attendants to wait on you; Tipping all nine for a guinea is as common there as two farthings for a porrenger of barley-broth at the hospital gate in Smithfield. . . . About five in the evening we went to see a great match at bowling. There was Quality and Reverend Doctors of both professions, Topping Merchants, Broken Bankers, Noted Mercers, Inns of Court Rakes, City Beaus, Stray'd Prentices and Dancing Masters in abundance. Fly, fly, fly, fly, said one. Rub, rub, rub, rub, cried another; ten guineas to five I uncover the Jack says a third. . . . From hence, we went to the Groom Porters, where they were a labouring like so many anchor smiths, at the Oak, Back-Gammon, Tick Tack, Basset, and throwing of Mains. There was palming, lodging, loaded dice, levant, and Gammoning with all the speed imaginable; but the Cornish rook was too hard for them all. The Bristol Fair sparks had but a very bad bargain of it, and little occasion for returns. . . . Having satisfied our curiosity here, we left them as busy a shaking their elbows as the apple-women in Stocks Market walnuts in October. And meeting with three or four more acquaintance, we strol'd to a Bristol Milk Dairy House and enjoy'd ourselves like brave Bacchanalians.

11 The Laughing Audience
From the painting by William Hogarth

12 The Masked Ball at the Wanstead Assembly
A study for a painting by William Hogarth

It was Nash's wish that life at these places should be communal and democratic. He did not encourage private parties or receptions at the lodgings of the visitors. Everything was to be done in public, and all classes were to mix without regard to their social position at home. In this he was obeyed, and while one class found the mixing amusing, another found it gratifying. The gaming-table, like the turf, is a great leveller, and Nash insisted that the ball-room should be likewise. The ball would be opened by the man of highest rank leading out the lady of the highest rank, but after that the man of rank was expected to dance with the grocer's daughter, and the lady with the shop-keeper. One of the lampoons of the time makes a point of this democratic, and at that time unusual, fusion of classes:

> Dressed as fine as modern beau,
> I the other night must go
> To the rooms, the throng to view,
> How I wished, dear Jack, for you.
>
> There I saw the peer, and knave,
> Commoner, and cringing slave,
> Bob-wig artists, ma'amoiselles,
> Shopkeepers, and abigails,
>
> Mixing, jostling each among
> (All seemed *equal* in the throng)
> Poor and affluent, great and small,
> Distinction levelled 'mongst them all.

In other country towns night-life centred on the local inn and the assembly-room, or the county-town house of the lords of the neighbouring country. The theatre, as at Bath, made little appeal, though in those days many a little town, which never to-day sees a play, was visited by strolling companies for a week, and sometimes more if the support was sufficient to give the members food and beds. Colley Cibber's scapegrace daughter, Charlotte (Charke), has given in her autobiography some piquant details of the minor theatre in the thirties and forties of the eighteenth century, and of the many mischances that beset the strolling player. There seems to have been no general law governing dramatic performances; the players were dependent entirely upon the whim of the local justice, and sometimes they were allowed to play, and sometimes not; and sometimes they even dared to play where performances were forbidden.

Thus, being once at Bristol, and almost penniless, Charlotte decided to give a performance and announce it as her benefit night, but "all was to be done under the rose, on account of the Magistrates, who have not suffered any plays to be acted in the city for many years, but notwithstanding I slily adventured to have *Barnwell* exhibited in the very heart of it, at the Black Raven, in High Street." The small town of Dartford had a curious law of its own, made perhaps with the idea that the common people should not be tempted from their work too early in the evening. Charlotte had an offer of a part in a small company playing at Dartford, and being penniless (again) she set out from London at three in the afternoon and walked to Dartford. She reached it by eight in the evening and "I played that night, for 'tis losing their Charter to begin before nine or ten."

It is odd that while Bristol could see no theatrical performances, Charlotte and her company played often in such small towns as Bradford-on-Avon, Honiton, Cullompton, Devizes, Lymington, Fareham, Cirencester, Chippenham, Corsham, Tiverton. The takings at most of these places afforded just enough to provide the company with a supper, and the audiences were what might be expected:

> At length the bespoke play was to be enacted, which was *The Beaux' Stratagem*; but such an audience, I dare believe, was never heard of before or since. In the first row of the pit sat a range of drunken butchers, some of whom soon entertained us with the inharmonious musick of their nostrils. Behind them were seated, as I suppose, their unsizable consorts, who seemed to enjoy the same state of happiness their dear spouses were possessed of; but having more vivacity than the males, laugh'd and talked louder than the players. . . . We both took a wild-goose chace through all the dramatic authors we could recollect, taking care not to let any single speech bear in the answer the least affinity; and while I was making love from Jaffier, she tenderly approved my passion with the soliloquy from *Cato*. In this incoherent manner we finished the night's entertainment. Mrs. Sullen, instead of Archer, concluding the play with *Jane Shore's* tag at the end of the first act of that tragedy, to the universal satisfaction of that part of the audience who were awake, and were the reeling conductors of those who only dreamt of what they should have seen.

The players were little better than the audiences. She says that most of the strolling companies she worked with were without any dramatic ability. The manager and manageress might be old-time professionals, but the rank-and-file were mainly apprentices and servants out of place with no stage experience at all, and no knowledge of how to move and speak. The wardrobe consisted of anything that could be picked up at auctions of the effects of derelict companies. A little earlier Steele had said much the same of the country strollers:

> We have now in this place a company of strollers, who are very far from offending in the impertinent splendour of the drama. They are so far from

falling into these false gallantries that the stage is here in its original situation of a cart. Alexander the Great was acted by a fellow in a paper cravat. The next day the Earl of Essex seemed to have no distress but his poverty; and my Lord Foppington the same morning wanted any better means to show himself a Fop Man by wearing stockings of different colours. In a word, tho' they have had a full barn for many days together, our itinerants are still so wretchedly poor that without you can prevail to send us the furniture you forbid at the play-house, the heroes appear only like sturdy beggars and the heroines gipsies.

Charlotte's night adventures at the little Gloucestershire town of Minchinhampton throw another light on the life of the strolling player of those days. When dramatic performances were illegal, it was open to anybody to inform, and to procure the arrest of the company as rogues and vagabonds, and receive a reward. In this case their landlord denounced them, and Charlotte and two men of the company were arrested and taken to prison. They were arrested at nine o'clock one morning, and kept in prison till nine the next morning:

> The evening wore apace, and the clock struck eight, the dreadful signal for the gates to be lock'd up for the night. I offered half a guinea apiece for beds, but was denied them; and, if I had not fortunately been acquainted with the turnkey, who was a very good-natured fellow, we must have been turn'd into a place to lie upon the bare ground, and have mixed among the felons, whose chains were rattling all night long, and made the most hideous noise I ever heard, there being upwards of two hundred men and boys under the different sentences of death and transportation.

After storming and demanding and wheedling, Charlotte and her friends finally got the use of the women's condemned-hole, in which two debtors were confined, who agreed for a consideration to sleep in the main hall. They were allowed to send for candles and wine, and somehow managed to make a night of it:

> I continued for the most part of the night very low spirited and in very ill humour, till I was roused by the drollery of one Mr. Maxfield, my fellow-sufferer, a good-natured man, and of an odd turn of humour; who would not let me indulge my melancholy, which he saw had strongly possessed me, and insisted, as he had often seen me exhibit Captain Macheath in a sham prison, I should, as I was then actually in the Condemned Hold, sing all the bead-roll of songs in the last act, that he might have the pleasure of saying I had once performed In Character. I own I was not in a condition to be cheerful, but the tender concern of those about me laid a kind of constraint on me to throw off my chagrin, and comply with their request.

Night-life at the spas other than Bath, and at the wells such as Epsom, Tunbridge, Bristol, was, during the eighteenth century, the same as at Bath. The Bath season ended in May, and in the middle and later years it was the custom for people to go on to Tunbridge Wells, Scarborough, or Harrogate. In 1761 Brighthelmstone was beginning to attract visitors, and a pamphlet by a medical man at that time spoke of its excellent air, and its waters, "particularly a mineral one." The pamphlet stated that two public rooms had been erected. One is described as convenient; the other as "not only so, but elegant; not excelled perhaps by any public room in England, that of York excepted; and the attention of the proprietor in preparing everything that may answer for the convenience and amusement of the company is extremely meritorious." But the amusement was all of a pattern, and followed that which was sketched in a popular play, *Tunbridge Walks*:

> "But what are the chief diversions here?"
> "Each to his own inclination—Beaus raffle and dance—Cits play at ninepins, bowls, and backgammon—Rakes scour the walks, bully the shop-keepers, and beat the fiddlers—Men of wit rally over claret, and fools get to the Royal Oak lottery, where you may lose fifty guineas in a moment, have a crown returned to you for coach hire, a glass of wine, and a hearty welcome."

Many contemporary pamphlets speak acidly of the monotony of the life and its unvarying evening round of tea, scandal, whist, quadrille, dances, assemblies, raffles and masquerades. Pope, Walpole, Lady Mary Wortley Montagu, and Smollett (in his own person) all refer to the pleasure of leaving Bath as being much greater than that of going to it, and an anonymous versifier sums up its diversions in two lines:

> 'Tis noise and nonsense are their dear delight,
> And stupid pleasures crown the drunken night.

Yet Smollett allowed one of the characters of his *Humphrey Clinker* to find its life full of interest:

> I think those people are unreasonable who complain that Bath is a contracted circle, in which the same dull scenes revolve without variation.... Here, for example, a man has daily opportunities for seeing the most remarkable characters of the community.... Here we have ministers of state, judges, generals, bishops, projectors, philosophers, wits, poets, players, chemists, fiddlers, and buffoons.... Another entertainment peculiar to Bath arises from the general mixture of all degrees assembled in our public rooms without distinction of rank or fortune.... I was extremely diverted, last ball night, to see the master of the ceremonies leading with great solemnity to the upper end of the room, an antiquated abigail, dressed in her lady's cast clothes; whom he, I suppose, mistook for some countess just arrived at the Bath. The ball was opened by a Scotch lord, with a mulatto heiress from St. Christopher's; and the gay Colonel Tinsel danced all the evening with the daughter of an eminent tinman from the borough of Southwark.

Night-life for the country workers of that time was, as in earlier years, limited to the village ale-house and the sing-song—a more sensible and spirited diversion anyhow than sitting glumly on the benches of the Dog and Duck, listening like a regiment to machine-made song and dance. Theirs was a communal life but it had its recreation devised and directed, not from above, but by themselves. They knew what they wanted, and they were not at all amenable to other people's ideas of what they ought to want. Their songs were made in or around their own village, and concerted in the tap-room of their own inn:

> Where wine and English liquors brew'd
> Of malt were sold for human good,
> Which drew the rural slaves from plough,
> From treading Hey and Barley-Mow,
> And swains and shepherds from their herds,
> With sunburnt looks and bristled beards,
> To wet their whistles with the liquor,
> And make their heavy souls the quicker.
> A crowd of these were got together,
> With faces tanned like bullocks' leather,
> Roaring out country songs and catches
> Over their belly jugs and gotches;
> Sometimes The Children in the Wood
> Was sung, till some both cry'd and spew'd;
> And then The Pie Sat in the Pear-tree,
> Was bawl'd so loud it would have fear'd ye,
> And when that good old ditty's done,
> The Fox, We'll Catch Him, Boys, Anon.
> As they were thus in merry mood,
> Consuming malt for th' public good,
> The fiddler . . .
> Was courting in a room hard by,
> Dandling his mistress on his thigh,
> And to engage her fickle mind,
> Was singing Oh, My Dear, My Kind . . .

Readers of *Peregrine Pickle* will remember the country ale-house club made up of Commodore Trunnion, Lieutenant Hatchway, Tom Pipes, the bo'sun's mate, and Mr. Pickle, and their two cans of rumbo apiece. Each evening, before entering the house, the Commodore would demand of the landlord if he had any attorneys aboard, and would not go in unless the answer was No. Once in, they took their rumbo ceremoniously, the newspaper was read aloud, with fierce comments from the Commodore, and the evening was passed in fighting sea-battles over again, and ended in song. Somewhere about the middle of each evening the lieutenant would bait the Commodore, and the Commodore would swing up his crutch to bring it down on the lieutenant's head, and the lieutenant would lift his wooden leg and parry the blow "to the no small admiration of Mr. Pickle, and utter astonishment of the landlord, who, by the bye, had expressed the same amazement, at the same feat, at the same hour, every night for three months before." Then the Commodore would order the bo'sun's mate to sound the whistle and give a song:

> The prelude being thus executed, Pipes fixed his eyes upon the egg of an ostrich that depended from the ceiling, and, without moving them from that object, performed the whole cantata in a tone of voice that seemed to be the joint issue of an Irish bagpipe and a sow-gelder's horn; the commodore, the lieutenant, and landlord joined in the chorus, repeating this elegant stanza:
>
> > Bustle, bustle, brave boys,
> > Let us sing, let us toil,
> > And drink all the while,
> > Since labour's the price of our joys.
>
> The third line was no sooner pronounced than the can was lifted to every man's mouth with admirable uniformity; and the next word taken up at the end of their draught with a twang equally expressive and harmonious. In short, the company began to understand one another; Mr. Pickle seemed to relish the entertainment, and a correspondence immediately commenced between him and Trunnion, who shook him by the hand, drank to further acquaintance and even invited him to a mess of pork and peas in the garrison. The compliment was returned, good fellowship prevailed, and the night was pretty far advanced when the merchant's man arrived with a lanthorn to light his master home.

Those were innocent enough revelries. The night pranks of many squires of those days, as presented by the novelists and dramatists, were, in comparison, sour and squalid. Fielding knew the country life of his time, and, while one allows for a little exaggeration, his portraits of one kind of squire were not invention. Squire Western was undoubtedly a contemporary type, not of all squires but of a considerable company. At that time they did not call themselves The County, and they were not ranked with aristocracy. There was a line as marked between the peerage of a county and its squires as between the merchant and his clerk. The evenings of many of those squires were passed usually with drink and horseplay. There were of course, the Squire Allworthys, but as they were reserved and decent people they received little attention from the novelists or even diarists.

Readers of *Joseph Andrews* will remember the fox-hunting squire encountered by Parson Adams. The squire invited him and Joseph and Fanny to dinner at his house, intending to have "sport" with the parson, to make Andrews drunk, and to get Fanny to himself. When they sat down to dinner, Adams was asked to say grace, and while he was saying it, one of the company removed his chair, and he sat on the floor. Another of the company overturned a plate of soup into his lap. The manservant put gin into his ale. A poet among the company composed and read a lampoon on him. A captain pinned a cracker to the parson's cassock, and lighted it with a candle. After a pretence of apology for these tricks, the parson was invited to read one of his sermons from a seat on a little platform at the end of the room. The seat was covered

A Village Assembly
From a caricature by Mathew Darly

by a large rug, and on either side of it two of the company sat as supporters. When the parson took his seat, the supporters rose from theirs, and the rug, which had no seat at its centre, was left loose, and the parson fell into a large tub of water set beneath it.

That was fiction, but there are enough records of certain squires of that time to show that horseplay was the basis of their evening diversions. The middle and professional classes in the country kept late hours, but in as quiet and seemly a way as now. An example of this was the music clubs of Worcester, of which Fanny Burney's cousin Richard was President, and the balls at which he was M.C., and the concerts of which he was conductor. As he himself said, there would be no living in the country without those things. He was a young man of the period, who only began to live when the lights went on, and only went to bed when the cocks began to crow. He disliked bed, and considered the time spent in it as so much taken from his life.

Horace Walpole did not share that opinion, and while he followed the fashion of the time he did it with complaint. In a letter to Richard Bentley he describes one of his days in 1755. He was then Member for King's Lynn, and it seems to have been a custom, when the House rose, for members to go on to vast assemblies, vast suppers, and then to balls. He describes how he sat through debates from two in the afternoon till midnight; then home, to change and dine, and then to a ball which lasted till five in the morning:

> In short, the true definition of me is that I am a dancing senator. Not that I do dance, or do anything by being a senator, but I go to balls and the house of commons—to look on; and you will believe me when I tell you that I really think the former the more serious occupation of the two: at least, the performers are most in earnest.

Elsewhere he describes himself as an unwilling rake, sharing in all sorts of night amusements—sitting up till between two and three, playing loo; keeping a lady company on a terrace in the moonlight of two o'clock in the morning because her chair had not come; supping with Prince Edward till half-past three.

Those night-long entertainments were not restricted to men and matrons. Young men and girls of the fashionable and middle-class shared them. Fanny Burney at eighteen reports a dance at a clergyman's house where the dancing began at nine o'clock, and lasted till five, when it was too late (or too early) to find a hackney-coach, and she and the rest of the company sat and sang glees until the day really began. At Gloucester she attended another ball, where supper was served at two o'clock, and the company lingered over it with music and song. When they thought it time to retire, they rang for candles, but on opening the door of the supper room they found the passage in broad daylight.

Just before her time some new evening pastimes had been devised, such as the masquerade, the ridotto, the drum, the *belle assemblée*, the rout, the bazaar, the *fiera in mascherata*—a sort of bazaar in which the stall-holders wore fancy dress. There were also the Italian Opera and the evening concerts; and the gaming-rooms were still at work in every town, as they are to-day. The favourite characters for the masquerades were those which are still to be seen at fancy-dress affairs—nuns, Quakers, witches, Punches, shepherds and shepherdesses, harlequins, huntsmen, Persians, Turks, friars, Indian Queens, Amazons, Columbines, and so on. Those entertainments were held in London at the

13 The Cockpit
From the engraving by William Hogarth

14 A Midnight Modern Conversation
From the engraving by William Hogarth

15 "A Night Scene at Ranelagh": the attack on Dr. John Hills in May, 1752

Opera House, the Panton Street Rooms, Vauxhall and Ranelagh, Marylebone Gardens, and the Hampstead Assembly; and in the country at the assembly rooms attached to the chief inn of each county town. Refreshments appear to have been generous. Most places provided a side-table on the floor of the dancing room with trifles to sustain the company between dances—tarts, cheese-cakes, patties, junket, and all the wines. The supper room was usually in the basement, and while there was much complaint about the beggarly suppers provided at Vauxhall and Ranelagh, the wafer slices of ham and tongue, and the everlasting chicken, those at the Opera were handsomely done. Half the larder was laid out, and all the wine cellar; which was not always good for the young men or some of the young ladies. Usually some special setting was devised for each affair—Moorish, Chinese, Arcadian. Sometimes it was a forest or a garden—the borders were laid with mould and planted with shrubs and flowers or saplings. Sometimes there was extra entertainment; a dance by the *corps de ballet* of the Opera; or a new thrill, such as an awesome Druid sitting in an arbour and handing ambiguous verses to each woman who passed him.

La Belle Assemblée seems to have been a rather advanced affair for the age; we of to-day haven't yet come up with it. At least, I have never heard of people paying for admission to a hall to sit and hear a number of ladies debate on abstract topics. The drums and routs were, of course, merely evening rendezvous at public rooms, where people drank tea and walked up and down and quizzed each other. The Ridotto al Fresco was—but let Walpole describe one, which he does with his usual urbane asperity:

> There was what they call a *ridotto al fresco* at Vauxhall, for which one paid half a guinea, though, except some thousand more lamps and a covered passage all round the garden, which took off from the garden-hood, there was nothing better than on a common night. Mr. Conway and I set out from his house at eight o'clock; the tide and torrent of coaches was so prodigious that it was half an hour after nine before we got half way from Westminster Bridge. We then alighted; and after scrambling under bellies of horses, through wheels, and over posts and rails, we reached the gardens, where there were already many thousand persons. Nothing diverted me but a man in a Turk's dress and two nymphs in masquerade without masks, who sailed amongst the company, and, which was surprising, seemed to surprise nobody. . . . We walked twice round and were rejoiced to come away, though with the same difficulties as at our entrance; for we found three strings of coaches all along the road, who did not move half a foot in half an hour. There is to be a rival mob in the same way at Ranelagh to-morrow; for the greater the folly and imposition the greater is the crowd. I have suspended the vestimenta that were torn off my back to the god of repentance, and shall stay away.

The private entertainments of the wealthy were often as elaborate as the public shows, and often as badly managed. There was a Queen's Birthday ball, which Walpole attended, given by Elizabeth Chudleigh at her house facing the Park. A scaffold for fireworks had been set up in the Park just opposite the windows, and the guests were received in rooms purposely kept dark for the better effect of the fireworks. They remained in the dark for two hours. After the fireworks were done the guests were treated to another illuminated spectacle, which was set in the courtyard. This consisted of portraits of the King and Queen in painted oil-paper, with the rest of the Royal Family represented by upright pillars and symbolical figures—a ship for the prince, a bird of paradise for the princess, orange trees for the younger members; and, for a recently-dead infant princess, a cradle, illuminated, which, during the night, went off in a blaze of crackers.

When, in 1760, the famous Mrs. Cornelys took the town house of the Earl of Carlisle in Soho Square, and threw it open as an Assembly Rooms, or night-club, she offered London something new. Vauxhall and Ranelagh were largely dependent upon the weather, and they were outside the town. Mrs. Cornelys provided much the same kind of entertainment, but under cover, and in a superbly furnished mansion of which subscribers had the free run. She was the first night-club hostess, on a scale of magnificence not attempted in our own day. While she received a public assembly, her Rooms kept all the amenities and atmosphere of a private home. All the leaders of Fashion and Society were on her books, and hundreds of others. Soho Square was nightly jammed with the coaches of the "quality," and a visit to London was not considered as complete unless it included at least one attendance at the Rooms. At the fortnightly halls or masquerades "everybody" was to be seen there. Not to be there was to be "out of it."

The parties were on the lines of those given to-day at smart houses. That is, if you have a ball-room which will comfortably serve a hundred dancers, and a drawing-room in which eighty people can be at ease, you invite four hundred guests, so that most of them spend two hours getting up your staircase, and the rest of the evening in being the inner part of a sandwich. This ungainly jam is called a brilliant and successful party, and the model for it seems to be the assemblies held at Mrs. Cornelys' house between 1760 and 1776. Always they were crowded. At each of them the mob-spirit was as manifest as at Sadlers Wells. So far from being kept away by heat and crowd and struggle, from which the fastidious shrink, the great world enjoyed those discomforts. Among the names of her supporters were those of Royal dukes, and frequent figures at the receptions were the Duke of Richmond, Lady Hertford, Lady Pembroke, Duchess of Hamilton, Duke of Devonshire, Lady Stanhope, Horace Walpole, Duchess of Northumberland, and indeed almost all the peerage. Fanny Burney paid her first visit, in 1770, and was not too enthusiastic. She had heard so much that she expected much. She approved the magnificence of the rooms and the decorations, and the dresses of the company, but she found the place, despite its many rooms, overcrowded, and the ball-room so heated and so full that there was no room for anybody to dance. It was just something to look at, not something in which one could take part; and as an entertainment she found it disappointing. But Fanny was of the decent professional middle-class, and had no fashionable love of crowd and clamour.

Mrs. Cornelys offered, of course, other attractions—or at least, one gets hints of them. There was much drinking; there were gaming-rooms; there were concerts at which the songs were of a kind not usually sung in public; and though no definite evidence is available of other irregularities, there are veiled references to private rooms which could be hired. After a successful run of some ten years, the thing began to decline and criticism became more emphatic. Subscribers' tickets were transferable, and the quality of the company suffered a coarsening of tone. An element of rowdiness began to intrude. Women of the town were seen on the staircases. Residents of the Square made complaints of her Rooms as a public nuisance, and feeling against her began to grow until a summons was issued against her charging her with keeping a common disorderly house and with suffering "divers loose, idle, and disorderly persons, as well men as women, to be and remain during the whole night, rioting and otherwise misbehaving themselves."

A feeling got about the place that its day was passing. The summons hastened the end, but before that was issued, two portents had appeared: the Pantheon in Oxford Street, and Almack's. Each of these challenged her supremacy; the Pantheon more sharply than Almack's, since its note was nearer to that of her own establishment, and it was more public than Almack's, whose conditions of membership had social demarcations more rigid than she was in a position to make. Each of those places flourished in its respective sphere, while the Soho Rooms went down. After the summons, she was bankrupt, and the contents of the house were sold. But a year or two later, she re-appeared and re-opened the Rooms. But again she was sold up, and after a few more efforts to rehabilitate herself as London's chief purveyor of entertainment, "the female Heidegger," as Walpole called her, she died in a debtors' prison.

The opening of the Pantheon in 1772 took custom both from her and from Almack's. But Almack's was strong enough to meet any rivalry, and it outlived the Pantheon by many years.

Almack was a man from the North named McCall, who, for business purposes, inverted his name to the form that became so well known in social history. In 1765 he already kept a club for men in Pall Mall, under his new name. (It afterwards became Brooks', and moved into St. James Street). It was, like White's, noted for its betting and gambling; its high stakes—nobody could play unless he kept a minimum of fifty guineas on the table—and the huge losses and winnings of the players. When this club was well floated and prospering, he looked around for something new, and conceived the idea of a better sort of Cornelys Rooms, run, not by himself but by a committee of men and women of unimpeachable position and integrity. This was the institution for which he built the Rooms in King Street, still to be seen (though a bomb fell quite near them in 1940) known as Willis's Rooms, and used as auction rooms. Almack's was at first just a subscription-room for balls, masquerades, and suppers once a week. Then a group of women formed a club of both sexes, and took part of the premises as their club-rooms, and became identified with the original scheme.

The rules of the establishment were that the men candidates for membership should be elected or refused by the committee of women, and the women candidates by the committee of men; so that no woman should be able to say that she had been excluded by the cattiness of a rival, and no man that he was barred by male jealousy. The ladies' committee, on its foundation, consisted of Lady Pembroke, Mrs. Fitzroy, Mrs. Meynell, Lady Molyneux, Miss Pelham and Miss Lloyd. Every name submitted for membership was scrutinised as severely as though it were a submission for Holy Orders. No name that was not socially perfect (morals didn't enter into it) could pass, and no second application was possible. Among those excluded were more than one peer; and the men's committee excluded the Duchess of Bedford of that time and other distinguished peeresses. Members had the privilege of taking a guest to the balls, but the guest likewise had to pass under the microscope. He or she had to call personally at the Rooms to receive either the Stranger's ticket of admission or a letter of refusal.

The Rooms of the club were open for dinner, and there was high play at cards, in which the men and women members joined. But its real life came at a later hour, with dancing and supper. Supper was served at eleven, and at that hour the doors were closed and no member, however high and mighty, could then be admitted. Dancing lasted till about dawn.

16 Vauxhall Gardens: Madame Weischel singing to a Distinguished Company
From a print by Thomas Rowlandson

17 "A Promenade at Carlisle House, Soho Square"
A Crayon Drawing of Mrs. Cornelys' famous establishment, by John Raphael Smith

18 "Dressing for the Ball"
From a drawing by Thomas Rowlandson

Almack's had a life of just on eighty years, and its most brilliant period was not at its foundation or at any time of the eighteenth century. It became what everybody thinks of when Almack's is mentioned, it became the most exclusive of all gatherings past or present—more exclusive than the Court—in the early years of the nineteenth century. It was not then a club or an Assembly Room. It was a place—*the* place —for dancing, and its weekly balls during the season were the chief social feature of each season. Only the most carefully sifted of even the *élite* were admitted, and the dragons of that day were even more severe and inexorable than the first committee. This exclusiveness was, of course, eventually its death, as exclusiveness always is. Its last years were rather a hanging-on than a being. The childish idea that the best of all England consisted of people who were "born," and that all others were Untouchables, could hardly survive under the running-to-seed of the old families and the triumph of the middle classes. The old families, having sicklied themselves by generations of inter-marriage, were compelled, for self-preservation, to marry their sons and daughters into the scorned world of "trade," and Almack's, in the forties of last century, faded from the scene so quietly that when it passed few people were aware that it was still alive.

In the third quarter of the eighteenth century the Cornelys Rooms, Almack's, and the Pantheon were the evening resorts of the fashionable only, while Ranelagh and Vauxhall were frequented by both the fashionable and the common citizens. Johnson often diverted his melancholy at these places, and Boswell records one or two utterances upon them. At a first visit to the Pantheon Boswell said that there was not half-a-guinea's worth of pleasure in seeing it. "But, sir," said Johnson, "there is half-a-guinea's worth of inferiority to other people in not having seen it." Boswell went on moralising: "I doubt, sir, whether there are many happy people here." "Yes, sir, there are many happy people here. There are people here who are watching hundreds, and who think hundreds are watching them. . . . I am a great friend to public amusements; for they keep people from vice. You now would have been with a wench had you not been here."

But when talking of Ranelagh he contradicted his remark about happy people. Boswell, in some connection, said that things were generally done upon the supposition of happiness; grand houses were built, fine gardens were made, splendid places of public amusement were contrived and crowded with company. "Alas, sir," said Johnson, "these are all only struggles for happiness. When I first entered Ranelagh, it gave an expansion and gay sensation to my mind such as I never experienced anywhere else. But as Xerxes wept when he viewed his immense army, and considered that not one of that great multitude would be alive a hundred years afterwards, so it went to my heart to consider that there was not one in all that brilliant circle that was not afraid to go home and think."

At those places the prosperous tradesman made as much a figure as those of the smart world. Citizens, tailors, lady's-maids, perruquiers, mixed in the walks and the Rotunda with princes and dukes. But they usually had the early hours of the evening to themselves; the real nobility, and those who wished to be thought to belong to it, did not arrive till about an hour before midnight, when the concert and the fireworks were over. The pretence of withdrawal and aloofness, of finding no pleasure in things that please everybody, was then a very general attitude. We have to-day perhaps gone a little too far in the opposite direction. It is now something of a fashion among the advanced to do all the mob things—to read crude mob-newspapers, to go to idiotic film-shows, to weigh the respective merits of musically illiterate dance-bands, and to cultivate roundabouts and fruit-machines.

The contempt of the eighteenth-century Quality (and sham-Quality) for popular pleasures is presented in one of the sketches in Goldsmith's *Citizen of the World*. The supposed Chinese author of the sketches is taken by a friend to Vauxhall, in the company of Beau Tibbs, Mrs. Tibbs, and a pawnbroker's widow:

> The illuminations began before we arrived, and I must confess that upon entering the gardens I found every sense overpaid with more than expected pleasure: the lights everywhere glimmering through the scarcely moving trees; the full-bodied concert bursting on the stillness of the night, the natural concert of the birds in the more retired part of the grove vying with that which was formed by art; the company gaily dressed, looking satisfaction, and the tables spread with various delicacies—all conspired to fill my imagination with the visionary happiness of the Arabian lawgiver, and lifted me into an ecstasy of admiration.

The company debate how they shall spend the evening, when the pawnbroker's widow finds herself in trouble. She has come prepared to enjoy whatever Vauxhall has to offer, and is reproved by Mrs. Tibbs for her ill-breeding. Mrs. Tibbs proposed keeping to the genteel walk of the garden, where there was always the best company. The widow wanted to get a good standing-place for seeing the waterworks or cascade—an illuminated mechanical side-show. Mrs. Tibbs made remarks about the widow's ideas belonging to behind the counter; and the widow retorted that some people could sit behind counters and still carve three good

19 The Interior of the Great Rotunda at Ranelagh
From a painting by Canaletto

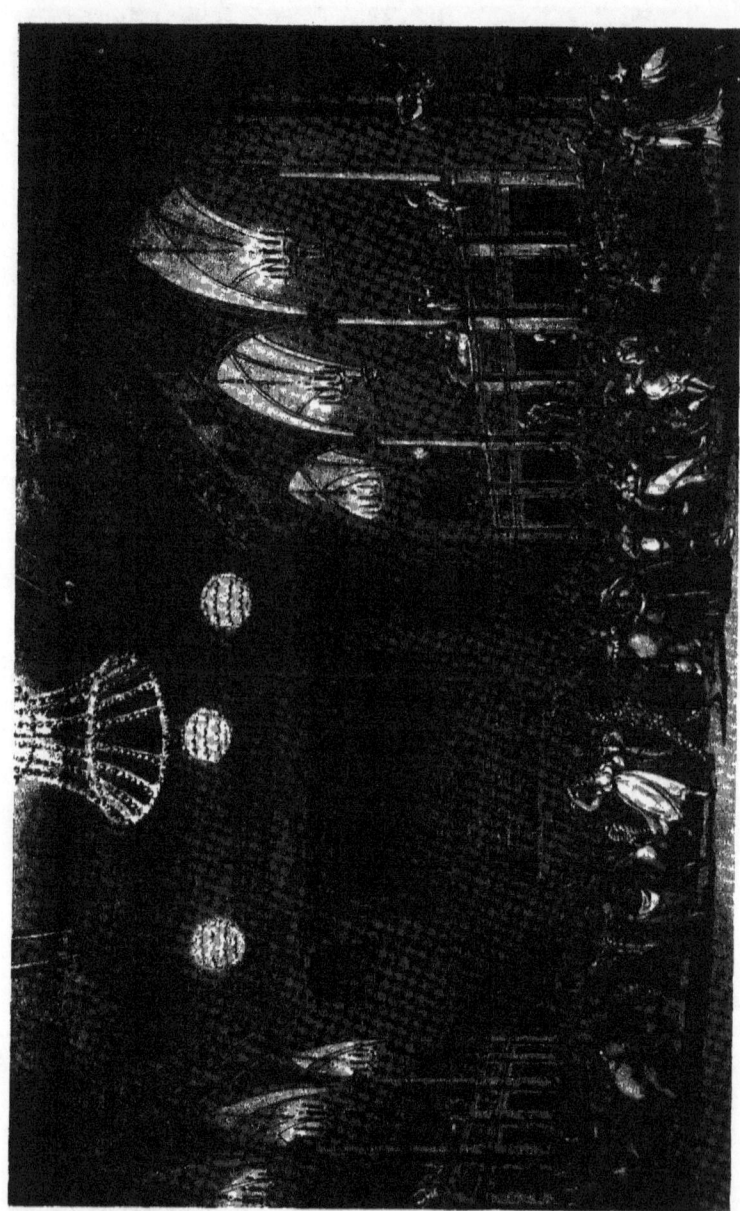

20 A Pantheon Masquerade
From the Rowlandson and Pugin print of 1809

joints of meat at their tables, while others hardly knew a rabbit and onions from a green goose and gooseberries. They compromised by going to one of the arbours for supper, where the widow found the meal excellent, and Mrs. Tibbs found it detestable, and Beau Tibbs thought the wine abominable:

> By this last contradiction the widow was fairly conquered in point of politeness. She perceived now that she had no pretensions in the world to taste; her very senses were vulgar, since she had praised detestable custard, and smacked at wretched wine; she was therefore content to yield the victory, and for the rest of the night to listen and improve. It is true she would now and then forget herself, and confess she was pleased, but they soon brought her back again to miserable refinement.

Nocturnal entertainment for the poorer people was provided at all sorts of gardens and springs of a humbler kind than Vauxhall and Ranelagh. Favourite evening resorts of clerks, apprentices, milliners and sempstresses, as well as those who were rather delicately called strolling damsels, were Cuper's Gardens, which stood where Waterloo Bridge meets Waterloo Road; the Dog and Duck, at St. George's Fields, the Temple of Flora and the Temple of Apollo, in the same district; and on the north of the river, Sadler's Wells, Bagnigge Wells, Belsize House, White Conduit House and a number of others. To encourage those who might be kept away by fear of dark roads and footpads, they advertised the provision of patrols and escorts:

> Patrols of horse and foot are stationed from Sadler's Wells' gate along the New Road to Tottenham Court Turnpike; likewise from the City Road to Moorfields; also from St. John Street, and across the Spa Fields to Rosoman Row.

Belsize House advertised that it kept twelve armed men always at hand to escort the timid, and Marylebone Gardens provided similar patrols.

Many of these gardens were open on Sundays, though no later than nine o'clock. Quiet games could be played—bowls, skittles, and so on— and religious scruples were observed by restricting the musical entertainment to performances on the organ. The entertainment, apart from concerts, was rather that of the kind one sees at fairs—dexterous people doing simple things in conditions of difficulty. A man would play a march on a flute while riding in standing position on two horses. Another would pick up one hundred eggs, each a yard from its neighbour, within an hour and fifteen minutes. Another would stand upright on horseback, and ride round a course, with a mask of bees on his face, and would fire a pistol and make half the bees swarm in the air and the other half perform some other trick. For a small fee you could be fastened by the neck in the pillory and be kissed in that position by one of the girl attendants.

Sometimes the entertainment took the form of a small Zoo; sometimes it was a giant or giantess. One side-turn that was immensely popular was a clever bit of showmanship on the part of the manager. Even our own publicising generation, which drags everything, general and private, into the High Street, has not, I think, had the idea of getting military heroes to repeat their glorious acts in public—to fight in mimic their battles o'er again. That was the point of this popular turn. An elderly soldier, who had been a drummer-boy at the battle of Malplaquet, and had helped a tight situation by beating what was called a Trevally under fire at the side of Marlborough, was engaged to beat that same Trevally on his old drum. The account does not state whether the management provided realism in the form of a few sharpshooters.

The entertainments and change of programme at the various gardens were regularly reported in the newspapers and periodicals of the time, and the reports are sometimes such obvious puffs, whether they appear as editorials or as Letters to the Editor, that one surmises they were paid for at advertisement rates. Thus, somebody writes to the Editor of the *Daily Advertiser* to report that, walking home one night to Islington, he was tempted to stop at a certain tavern-garden in Coldbath Fields, where he found excellent beer, beautifully illuminated grounds, and a concert both vocal and instrumental, all (including the beer) for threepence.

Another public-spirited citizen draws attention to the amusement provided at the Sir John Oldcastle, and expresses his delight at the show given by the Three Bath Morris Dancers, in such terms that he must have been one of them or perhaps their manager or press-agent. At Phillips New Wells, in Clerkenwell, you could see, for the price of your pint of wine, an entertainment by a company of English, French, and German performers:

> This evening will be performed several new exercises of rope-dancing, tumbling, vaulting, equilibres, ladder-dancing, and balancing by Madame Kerman, Sampson, Rogetzi, Monsieur German and Monsieur Dominique; with a new grand dance, called Apollo and Daphne, by Mr. Phillips, Mrs. Lebrune and others; singing by Mrs. Phillips and Mrs. Jackson; likewise the extraordinary performance of Herr von Eeckenberg, who imitates the lark, thrush, blackbird, goldfinch, canary-bird, flageolet, and German flute; a sailor's dance by Mr. Phillips, and Monsieur Dominique flies through a hogshead, and forces both heads out. To which will be added The Harlot's Progress.

Surely, after so much richness, rather an anti-climax.

21 A Gaming-house in Covent Garden
From an engraving of 1746

22 Night
From the engraving by William Hogarth

23 Early Morning
From the engraving by William Hogarth

24 A Dispute in a Gaming-house
From an engraving of ca. 1740

25 A Dispute in a Theatre Lobby
From a late-Georgian print

The grosser pleasures of the town were much the same as they are to-day. The term "pub-crawl" had not been invented, but the thing itself was known, and one of Roderick Random's evenings—not unlike the evenings of our own Randoms—was just that.

He began at a coffee-house, and scraped acquaintance. The coffee-house served an ordinary in an upper room, and he joined the company at table, and shared in the conversation and disputes. England was at war, and the disputes have a curiously modern ring. Two or three of the company uttered sentiments about the then enemy (France) calculated to cause alarm and despondency in the hearts of Cabinet Ministers. An ex-officer censured the commanders of the Allied forces, and attacked the Ministry for employing people who had neither experience nor capacity. Another showed that the claim of Spain to the Austrian possessions in Italy was natural and right. Another that the French King's breaking of his contract on the Pragmatic Sanction was justified, since to have kept his word would have injured his own glory. Another held that the French and Spanish were altogether better than the English, and spoke of their conquests, the discipline of their troops, and the fact that they were better clothed and better fed than the English. A foreigner lauded the French system of government as far superior to that of England, and held that the French people were the happiest subjects in the world.

Whereupon the one patriot present let himself go in terms which have been heard pretty often in our police-courts during the last year. "You know very well that had you dared to speak so freely of the administration of your own country in Paris as you have done of ours in London, you would have been sent to the Bastille without ceremony. . . . We want not laws to chastise the authors of seditious discourses, and if I hear another word out of your mouth in contempt or prejudice of this kingdom . . ."

The company then returned to the coffee-room, and Roderick picked up an eccentric doctor, who invited him to join a party at the Bedford Coffee House in Covent Garden. Here, after being introduced to the party—a painter, a player, and three young men about town—he sat and talked with them on the weather, the latest plays, current politics, and other topics, until one of them proposed going on to another tavern close at hand. Here they took a private room, called for wine, and ordered a supper, when the party set about making the doctor the butt of the evening. The three young men became noisy; the player began to rehearse his new part; the painter "took off" the other members of the party; Roderick sang French catches; the doctor became sullen.

Then it was suggested that they should scour the district, sweat the constable, beat the watch, and "reel soberly to bed." But the young men had not finished with the doctor. The waiter, on their private instructions, introduced a woman of the town, who charged the doctor with being the father of her child. After violent protestation and denial, the doctor, on the advice of the company, satisfied her with half a guinea, when she asked for a parting kiss, and bit his cheek. The doctor, thinking she was mad, was alarmed by the possible consequences of the bite, and one of the young men suggested cauterising with a red-hot poker, while another volunteered to cut out the affected part with the point of his sword. But the painter recommended a balsam which he always carried, and thereupon produced a bottle of black paint, with which he daubed most of the doctor's face, who was then sent home in a chair.

They then turned to the player, who had made himself unpopular by trying to promote a quarrel, and set him to show his paces by leaping over their outstretched swords on pain of being pricked from behind if he were not nimble enough. Under compulsion, he performed the feat and fled, leaving them to pay his share of the reckoning.

By that time it was two o'clock, and they decided to move on to another haunt. But in the air of the street the party began to dissolve. The painter disappeared into the darkness. One of the young men was completely overcome, and they sent him in a chair to a bagnio. Roderick and the other two went to Moll King's coffee-house, or shed, which stood by the front of St. Paul's, Covent Garden (as shown in Hogarth's *Morning*), and there, after a time, one of them went to sleep on a bench, and Roderick and the other walked home to their lodgings at Charing Cross.

Moll King's was one of the most notorious of the Covent Garden houses. It was first known as Tom King's, but after his death his widow carried on the business and gave it her name. It was a one-room affair, with poor appointments and nothing to recommend it save its reputation. According to a contemporary writer, "noblemen and the first beaux after leaving Court would go to her house in full dress, with swords and bags, and in rich brocaded silk coats, and walk and converse with persons of every description. She would serve chimney-sweepers, gardeners, and the market people in common with lords of the highest rank." She was often indicted for keeping a disorderly house, and more than once stood in the pillory.

The Bedford Coffee House, where Roderick had his spree, was one of the best of the many coffee-houses in that district. It was "every night

26 "Frederick squandering away his Fortune at a Bagnio"
From an illustration of 1787

27 "The Countryman in London"
From an engraving of 1771

28 A late-Georgian Nocturne
From a print by H. Wigstead

crowded with men of parts. Almost everyone you meet is a polite scholar and a wit. Jokes and bon-mots are echoed from box to box." Among the nightly "regulars" at various times were Sam Foote, Henry Fielding, Arthur Murphy, Dr. Arne, Hogarth, Churchill, Goldsmith, Quin, Garrick, and William Collins.

Covent Garden, indeed, for about a century and a half, was the heart of London's night-life. The Piazza and the side-streets were thick with taverns, coffee-houses, vapour-bath houses, and scores of less reputable houses which described themselves as bagnios and so led to the term being dropped by the actual bathing-houses and becoming a synonym for brothel. Most of these places were open all night, both the illicit houses and the actual Hummums. The baths offered, as they do to-day, bedrooms for those who arrived late at night. An advertisement of the original Hummums (there was till lately a hotel of that name in the Market) makes a point of this:

> At the Hummums in Covent Garden are the best accommodation for persons of quality to sweat or bath every day in the week, the conveniences of all kinds far exceeding all other bagnios or sweating houses both for rich and poor. Persons of good reputation may be accommodated with handsome lodgings to lie all night.

In Long Acre was another Hummums which also provided beds and advertised the fact in a curiously-worded paragraph:

> There is no entertainment for women after twelve of the clock at night, but all gentlemen that desire beds may have them for two shillings a night ... which rooms and beds are fit for the entertainment of persons of the highest quality and gentlemen.

The distinction made in the last phrase may have been accidental, but at that time there was often room for such a distinction.

The Piazzas around the market were the nightly walk for women of the town, and it was a regular practice for rich rakes to sit in their coaches and watch the up-and-down procession until they saw a face that attracted them, when they would make a signal and the lady would join them. It was a district also of minor gaming-houses. It seems that during the eighteenth century any member of the peerage had the right to run a gaming-house, and some of them used a portion of their town-houses for this purpose. Etiquette was strict and the play was fair. Swords had to be left at the door. There was a silver table and a gold table, and attendants stood about the room to keep order and watch for sharpers. Stakes at the silver table were from a shilling upwards, and at the gold table from half a guinea. The company at the silver table was usually composed of shop-boys, apprentices, and lawyer's clerks. Those at the gold table were the habitual and professional plungers, with a few young squires, and sometimes a highwayman trying to increase by luck what he had acquired on the road by pluck.

A famous Covent Garden night-haunt which opened about that time, and was known up to the middle of the nineteenth century was the Cider Cellar, in Maiden Lane, otherwise known as the Midnight Concert

A London Night Haunt of the Eighteenth Century
From an early engraving by Hogarth

Room. It was actually a cellar, very plainly furnished, and cider was then its chief drink. Its entertainment was mainly in the nature of a free-and-easy sing-song, the landlord leading off, and then calling upon the "gemmen" to oblige. During the later years of the eighteenth century it was the favourite resort of Richard Porson, the "Grecian," who came at midnight and usually stayed till daybreak. Among those who shared its delights with him were John Moore and Captain Morris, the "Beefsteak" lyrist, who would bring a company from that club, or the Humbug club, or the Anacreontic club (there was no end to Morris's clubs) and finish the night there. The unpleasant notoriety which to-day attaches to its memory was not earned until early Victorian days, when

29 The Country Club
From a print by H. Bunbury

30 Reading the Newspaper in a London Coffee-house
From a print by H. Bunbury

31 The Morning After
From a drawing by Thomas Rowlandson

that odd character, Renton Nicholson, kept it and, by industry and perseverance, brought it to ruin.

A writer of the early nineteenth century, looking back fifty years, summed up Covent Garden and its haunts of that time in the usual spirit of nostalgia:

> The first beauties of the time assembled every evening under the Piazzas, and promenaded for hours . . . the gay scene partook of the splendour of a Venetian carnival, and such beauties as The Kitten, Peggy Yates, Sally Hall the brunette, Betsy Careless, graced the merry throng, with a hundred more, equally famed, whose names are enrolled in the cabinet of Love's votaries. Then there was a celebrated house in Charles Street, called the Field of Blood, where the droll fellows of the time used nightly to resort, and throw down whole regiments of black artillery; and then at Tom or Moll King's, a coffee house so called, which stood at the centre of Covent Garden market, at midnight might be found the bucks, bloods, demireps, and choice spirits of London, associated with the most elegant and fascinating Cyprians, congregated with every species of human kind that intemperance, idleness, necessity, or curiosity could assemble together.
>
> There you might see Tom King enter as rough as a Bridewell whipper, roaring down the long room and rousing all the sleepers, thrusting them and all who had empty glasses out of his house, setting everything to rights—when in would roll three or four jolly fellows, claret-cosey, and in three minutes put it all into uproar again; playing all sorts of mad pranks, until the guests in the long room were at battle-royal together. . . .

He mentions the Spiller's Head in Clare Market, whose sign the landlord changed from the Bull and Butcher in honour of one of his customers, James Spiller, the original Mat of the Mint of *The Beggar's Opera*. It drew much the same nightly company as the Bedford—Hogarth, Churchill, Garth, Wilkes, the Duke of Wharton. He speaks of a painting of Hogarth's, which was never engraved, showing the interior of the Spiller's Head at night. Its title was *St. James' Day*, the first day for oysters; and it shows an oyster-woman opening oysters for the Duke of Wharton, with the regular company at table and at the bar—Garth, Walker (the first Macheath), Lavinia Fenton (the first Polly) and others.

A club of a quite sedate kind, founded about 1755 in Bride Lane, exists and meets to this day, and thus has had a life of nearly two hundred years. This is the Society of Cogers—or thinkers. It was—and is—a debating society, somewhat on the lines of the original Mug House Club, in that the members sat at table with tankards or glasses, but without song. The topic for the weekly debate was usually some recent event in home or foreign politics. It had a President to regulate proceedings (Wilkes at one time had the office) and the first speaker had forty minutes, the first respondent fifteen minutes, and others were allowed ten minutes. This procedure has been consistently followed through the years, and is followed to-day at the Society's Saturday night meetings.

When clubs, in their constitution and purpose, were becoming more and more fantastic, it was inevitable that somebody would carry the fantastic to extremity. So came those outrageous night-clubs, called Hell-Fire Clubs. The chief of them was, of course, that founded by Sir Francis Dashwood at Medmenham, near West Wycombe—the Monks of Medmenham, who met in a building specially built by Dashwood in the form of a monastery. Exactly what went on at their meetings we do not know. There are various accounts which conflict with each other, and none of them is perhaps reliable; all seem to be based on hearsay. The most circumstantial account is that given by Charles Johnstone in his *Chrysal, or the Adventures of a Guinea*; a novel which surveys the social scene of the middle eighteenth century through a series of episodes supposed to be narrated by a golden guinea from its observations as it passes from hand to hand.

If his account is anywhere near the truth, the club meetings began with the celebration of the Black Mass, and ended in objectionable orgies. The cellars of the monastery "were stored with the choicest wines; the larders with the delicacies of every climate; and the cells were fitted up for all the purposes of lasciviousness, for which proper objects were also provided." The members were limited to twelve, after the number of the disciples, and each took the name of a disciple. And there were twelve probationary members to fill places left vacant by death or desertion. Among the members were the Earl of Sandwich, Bubb Doddington, John Wilkes, Robert Lloyd, the minor poet, and the Duke of Wharton.

According to Johnstone, the rites and pleasures of the society were of such a nature that if they had been habitual no constitution could have supported them. For this reason, and to maintain them in their first freshness, meetings were held only twice a year and lasted only for a week. The proceedings began with a dinner, and after dinner the "monks" retired to their cells to put on their robes and prepare for the travesty of a religious service, which was held in the "chapel." This chapel had all the appearance of a normal chapel save in its mural and other decorations. The ceiling was covered with "emblems and devices too gross to require explanation to the meanest capacity, and the walls painted with the portraits of those whose names and characters they

assumed, represented in attitudes and actions horrible to imagination."
The ceremony for the initiation of a new candidate is thus described by Johnstone:

> My master then clad in a milk white robe of the finest linen that flowed loosely about him, repaired at the tolling of a bell to the chapel, the scene of all their mysterious rites, and knocking gently thrice at the door, it was opened to him to the sound of soft and solemn musick.
>
> On his entrance he made a most profound obeisance, and advancing slowly towards a table that stood against the wall, in the upper end of the chapel, as soon as he came to the rails, by which it was surrounded, he fell upon his knees, and making a profession of his principles, nearly in the words but with the most gross perversion of the sense of the articles of faith of the religion established in the country, demanded admission within the rails, the peculiar station of the upper order. . . . The superior then proceeded to take the suffrages of the rest with the same mimic solemnity; when my master being found to have the majority, his election was exultingly attributed to immediate inspiration, and he was accordingly admitted within the rails, where he received the name and character which he was to bear in the society, in a manner not proper to be described, every the most sacred rite and ceremony of religion being profaned, all the prayers and hymns of praise appointed for the worship of the Deity burlesqued by a perversion to the horrid occasion.

When these ceremonies were done, supper was served in the chapel. It was laid and attended by the probationary members. Sir Francis dared not allow the domestics of his own establishment to see his monastery and its contents, so only the two dozen knew its secrets, and all cleaning and preparation were done by the probationers. At the supper:

> Nothing that the most refined luxury, the most lascivious imagination could suggest to kindle loose desire, and provoke and gratify appetite, was wanting, both the superiors and the inferiors (who were permitted to take their places at the lower end of the table, as soon as they had served in the banquet) vying with each other in loose songs and dissertations of such gross lewdness and daring impiety as despair may be supposed to dictate to the damned.

After supper, there was a solemn invocation to Satan to come among them and receive their adoration; and then they retired to their individual pleasures, for which provision had previously been made. He gives no description of the Black Mass of invocation, but it no doubt followed the old form described in our own time by Huysmans in *Là-bas*.

A notable devotee of night-life, though of a placid kind, was Samuel Johnson. He shared young Burney's dislike of bed, but he equally disliked getting up. He told Boswell that he usually rose late, went out at four o'clock for dinner, and seldom got home before two. A friend of his, an assistant preacher at the Temple, gave Boswell a more precise account:

> About twelve o'clock I commonly visited him, and frequently found him in bed, or declaiming over his tea. . . . He generally had a levee of morning visitors, chiefly men of letters. . . . He declaimed all the morning, then went to dinner at a tavern, where he commonly stayed late, and then drank his tea at some friend's house, over which he loitered a great while, but seldom took supper. I fancy he must have read and wrote chiefly in the night, for I can scarcely recollect that he ever refused going with me to a tavern, and he often went to Ranelagh, which he deemed a place of innocent recreation. He frequently gave all the silver in his pocket to the poor, who watched him between his house and the tavern where he dined. He walked the streets at all hours, and said he was never robbed, for the rogues knew he had little money, nor had the appearance of having much.

Elsewhere, Boswell records one occasion when he did manage to rise early, or was made to rise by his friends. Topham Beauclerk and Bennet Langton had been making a night of it at a tavern, and at about three in the morning the alcoholic fancy came to them that Johnson might like to join them:

> They rapped violently at the door of his chambers in the Temple, till at last he appeared in his shirt, with his little black wig on the top of his head, instead of a night-cap, and a poker in his hand, imagining, probably, that some ruffians were coming to attack him. When he discovered who they were, and was told their errand, he smiled, and with great good humour agreed to their proposal: "What, is it you, you dogs! I'll have a frisk with you." He was soon drest, and they sallied forth together into Covent Garden, where the greengrocers and fruiterers were beginning to arrange their hampers, just come in from the country. Johnson made some attempts to help them; but the honest gardeners stared so at his figure and manner, and odd interference, that he soon saw his services were not relished. They then repaired to one of the neighbouring taverns, and made a bowl of that liquor called Bishop, which Johnson had always liked; while in joyous contempt of sleep, from which he had been roused, he repeated the festive lines:
>
>> Short, O short then be thy reign,
>> And give us to the world again!

After this they walked down to the river and rowed to Billingsgate. We are not told whether Johnson made similar clumsy attempts to be helpful with the fish; Boswell says only that they were so pleased with their amusement "that they resolved to persevere in dissipation for the rest of the day." When Garrick heard of the little spree, he warned Johnson that the newspapers would get hold of it. But Johnson was a little uppish about it: "*He* durst not do such a thing. His wife would not let him!"

His four clubs, and the midnight conversation they inspired, were such as are hardly known in our time, when scarcely any club maintains its original "note." Also, while the day still has twenty-four hours, few people have the time for composed talk or for any talk except unparseable and dishevelled sentences of half a dozen words. There was, first, the Ivy Lane Club (off Pasternoter Row); then, in 1764, the famous Literary Club; in 1780 the City Club, held at the Queen's Arms, St. Paul's Churchyard; and the last was Sam's, or the Essex Head Club, held at a tavern of that name in Essex Street kept by an old servant of Thrale's, Samuel Greaves.

One of Sir John Hawkins' anecdotes of the Ivy Lane Club illustrates Johnson's love of the midnight hours for social recreation. When the first book of his friend Charlotte Lennox was published, he proposed to celebrate it by an all-night gathering of the Club at a more commodious tavern. They chose the Devil, in Fleet Street, and at eight o'clock the authoress and another lady, and one or two men friends, as well as the members of the Club, met there for supper:

> Our supper was elegant, and Johnson had directed that a magnificent hot apple-pye should make a part of it, and this he would have stuck with bay-leaves, because, forsooth, Mrs. Lennox was an authoress, and had written verses; and further, he had prepared for her a crown of laurel, with which, but not until he had invoked the Muses by some ceremonies of his own invention, he encircled her brows. The night passed, as must be imagined, in pleasant conversation and harmless mirth, intermingled, at different periods, with the refreshments of coffee and tea. About five, Johnson's face shone with meridian splendour, though his drink had been only lemonade; but the far greater part of us had deserted the colours of Bacchus, and were with difficulty rallied to partake of a second refreshment of coffee, which was scarcely ended when the day began to dawn. This phenomenon began to put us in mind of our reckoning; but the waiters were all so overcome with sleep that it was two hours before we could get a bill, and it was not till near eight that the creaking of the street-door gave the signal for our departure.

The Literary Club, which met at the Turk's Head, in Gerrard Street, had a shining register of members. Among them were Joshua Reynolds (its founder), Johnson, Burke, Topham Beauclerk, Bennet Langton, and Goldsmith. Later members included Garrick, Gibbon, Adam Smith, Charles James Fox, Sheridan, Charles Burney, and Boswell. The talk among such an intelligent and piquantly assorted company must have been exceptionally good. Unfortunately Boswell gives only a few scraps of its proceedings, perhaps because it was still in existence at the time he wrote and many of the members were still living; and what is said at a club is held to be even more confidential than talk at a private table.

The Club was so successful that it went along on its own impetus. Its centenary was celebrated in 1864, when it was more aristocratic than literary; the members being then Lord Clarendon, Lord Stanhope, Lords Brougham, Stanley, Kingsdown, the Duke of Argyll, the Earl of Carlisle, Earl Russell, Lord Overstone, Lord Glenelg, and a string of bishops, knights, and hons. Somewhere among the full list, under the heap of coronets, one catches the names—Macaulay, Hallam, and George Grote.

The other clubs of Johnson died as their members died, or as the fashion changed from the intimate conversation-club, meeting three nights a week, to the large club with its own premises open from morning to morning.

A club to which he sometimes went, not of his own founding, was one of several Blue-Stocking Clubs. These, as described by Boswell, were evening assemblies at ladies' houses, "where the fair sex might participate in conversation with literary and ingenious men." The title, which came to mean what we to-day would call female highbrows, did not derive from women's dress or from any feminine association. It came, Boswell says, from a man, a natural-historian named Stillingfleet, who dressed very soberly and wore blue stockings. He was one of the best talkers at these assemblies; so much so that when he was not there the conversation flagged, and the ladies would cry "We can do nothing without Blue Stockings." Hannah More gave a description of one of these assemblies in her poem, *Bas-Bleu*, and Boswell has described one of the meetings at which he himself turned up merrily tight. Johnson, he says, went often to them, and engaged in lively banter with the ladies, as with Miss Monckton (later Countess of Cork) who held the best "bit of blue" at her mother's house, and whom he called a dunce for being affected by the writings of Laurence Sterne. When, later, she asked him to explain this, his answer was: "Madam, if I had thought so, I certainly should not have said it." Boswell's own breach of decorum needs his own words:

> I had dined at the Duke of Montrose's with a very agreeable party, and his Grace, according to his usual custom, had circulated the bottle very freely. Lord Graham and I went together to Miss Monckton's, where I certainly was in extraordinary spirits, and above all fear or awe. In the midst of a great number of persons of the first rank, amongst whom I recollect, with confusion, a noble lady of the most stately decorum, I placed myself next to Johnson, and thinking myself now fully his match, talked to him in a loud and boisterous manner, desirous to let the company know how I could contend with Ajax. I particularly remember pressing him upon the value of the pleasures of the imagination, and as an illustration of my argument, asking

him, "What, Sir, supposing I were to fancy that the —— (naming the most charming duchess in his Majesty's dominions) were in love with me, should I not be very happy?" My friend, with much address, evaded my interrogatories, and kept me as quiet as possible; but it may easily be conceived how he must have felt.

In the hope of putting it right, he made it rather worse by sending Miss Monckton a set of verses, suggesting that it was not so much wine as her bright eyes that had made him drunk, and not brilliantly drunk, but dully and smokily drunk. Which was hardly complimentary to the bright eyes.

Another of the Blue Stocking clubs met at the house of Elizabeth Montagu, who was really the leading spirit, if not the founder, of those groups. Stillingfleet was a member of that, too, and others were Horace Walpole, Lord Lyttleton, Elizabeth Carter (translator of Epictetus) and the Hon. Mrs. Boscawen and Mrs. Vesey. Other assemblies of a similar kind were held by Sir William Pepys, Mrs. Ord, and Mrs. Delany. Fanny Burney went to one or two, and found them more satisfying than the assemblies of Mrs. Cornelys. Her father told their hostess, and Fanny agreed, that it was gratifying to find houses where entertainment could be had without cards, music, or dancing. Of the ladies associated with those gatherings, the names recalled to-day when the term Blue Stocking is used (in the sense of learned ladies or *précieuses*) are Mrs. Montagu, Hannah More, Elizabeth Carter, and Mrs. Delany.

Pleasant nights were also had at Sir Joshua Reynolds', and Johnson was a regular visitor, usually after dinner. He held that dining was one thing, and talking another; and when Boswell complained that he had dined at a great house and heard not a single good remark at table, Johnson said that people gathered at table to eat and drink together, and to promote kindness, which was more easily done if there was no solid conversation; some of the company who were not capable of such conversation would be left out and would feel uneasy. And he added this illuminating light on table manners in Queen Anne's day, which shows that the loose dialogue of the dramatists was not as far removed from real life as some say it was—"It was for this reason, Sir Robert Walpole said, he always talked bawdy at his table, because *in that all could join*."

The discussions at Johnson's own clubs, so far as Boswell or Hawkins reports them, often became disputes, and the disputes often led to bad temper or sulks—which never happened at the Blue Stocking assemblies. The cause was almost always Johnson himself; his love of contradicting whatever had just been said—even if he himself had said something of the sort a month ago—and of over-riding any argument that put him wrong. In more than one passage Boswell accuses Goldsmith of a desire to "shine" in company. That desire seems equally to have been Johnson's; and not only to shine but to be supreme, and by any means. But however violently feelings were ruffled by the Johnson rudeness, it was a company of civilised men of letters. None of their disputes ended in weapons and death, as happened at a club of country gentlemen of that period—a period when the self-control of some of that class was not much above that of their own peasants.

It was at a dinner of the Nottinghamshire Club, at the Star and Garter tavern in Pall Mall, that Lord Byron, grand-uncle of the poet, killed his neighbour, Mr. Chaworth, in an affray following a dispute as to how many manors were owned by a mutual neighbour.

The club met once a month for dinner, usually towards the end of the month. Dinner began soon after four o'clock, and continued till seven, when the cloth was drawn, bottles were set on the table, and the evening went merrily. This particular dinner was at the end of January, and the company was as merry as usual until somebody started an argument on the best method of preserving game. This led Chaworth to say that Lord Byron, who took no trouble to preserve his game, would have none at all on his estate but for the care of himself and a neighbour, Sir Charles Sedley. Lord Byron then wanted to know how many manors Sedley owned, and Chaworth told him. Lord Byron pointed out that one of the manors mentioned was his own, whereupon Chaworth told him that if he wanted to know how many manors Sedley owned, he would find him in Dean Street, and could ask him; and as to himself (Chaworth) Lord Byron knew where to find him at any time.

Nothing more was said until the party broke up. Then, apparently, Chaworth and Lord Byron met on the staircase. The dining-room was on the second floor. They went down to the first floor, and asked a waiter for an empty room. The waiter showed them to a room, and left a lighted candle with them.

About three minutes later the bell of that room was sharply rung. The waiter went to answer it, entered the room, and ran down again to call the proprietor. The proprietor went up and found Chaworth and Lord Byron with drawn swords, Chaworth leaning heavily on Lord Byron's shoulder. Each man handed him his sword, and Chaworth was supported to a chair. Some members of the club then came in, and while awaiting the arrival of a doctor asked what had happened. Chaworth said that he had not long to live, and that he forgave Lord Byron. He added that Lord Byron had asked whether he had intended

32 "The Comforts of Bath": a Concert

33 "The Comforts of Bath": an Evening Reception

34 "Playing in Parts": a Musical Evening of 1801
From a print by James Gillray

his remarks about game to apply to Sir Charles Sedley or to himself, and that he had suggested that if there was to be any further discussion he would first shut the door. He went to do this, when Lord Byron called upon him to draw. He saw that Lord Byron was already drawing, and he drew his own sword an instant more quickly, and made a lunge at his opponent. The blade passed through Lord Byron's coat, and brought Chaworth close to him; whereupon Lord Byron shortened his sword and stabbed him in the stomach.

After attention from the doctor, Chaworth was removed to his London home, and died there the next day. Lord Byron was arrested and taken to the Tower, and three months later was tried by his peers. He was found Not Guilty of Murder, but Guilty of Manslaughter. As a peer, he pleaded Benefit of Clergy, and got clean off.

In the last quarter of the eighteenth century the music club and the free-and-easy song and drama club were a special feature of London night-life. Henry Angelo, the fencing-master, in his *Reminiscences*, mentions several of these. One was held at the Paul's Head tavern in the City; another at the Queen's Arms, in Newgate Street; and a third at the Jacob's Well, in Barbican. The concert club at the Queen's Head was composed partly of professionals and partly of amateurs. The general public was admitted to the weekly concerts at a charge of two shillings; after the concert, supper was served in the bar-parlour, and the company, audience and performers, would spend some hours in music-talk. The club at the Jacob's Well was apparently a club for young stage aspirants. "There," Angelo says, "the amateurs of fun and frolic might obtain a rich treat for the accustomed price of a broil, a Welch rabbit, and a glass of wine or spirits and water; and waste the night in glorious independence." He describes its proceedings as quite harmless in comparison with those of the Dog and Duck, which he calls a wholesale receptacle of vice, only rivalled in depravity by the Apollo Gardens and Bagnigge Wells.

At the Jacob's Well the evening was spent in speeches, songs, mimicry, declamation, and drollery. He describes an evening he spent there with one of the wildest of the bucks of the age, Lord Barrymore:

> Dining one day *tête-à-tête* with his lordship, and partaking of his bottle of claret, for want of better amusement, he started up and, ringing the bell, ordered his carriage, saying "Come, Harry Angelo, you and I will go and see the gay doings at Jacob's Well." We drove off, and arrived there about half-past nine, his lordship, to avoid being known as a great man, alighting at some distance. The long room, if I may depend on my memory, was on the ground floor, and all the benches were filled with motley groups, eating,

drinking, and smoking. . . . There was a president who, from a rostrum, knocking with his ivory mallet, hoarsely bawled "Will any gentleman favour the company with a speech, a recitation, an imitation, or a song?" Half a dozen candidates for fame, in each department proposed, started up; when the moderator, from his lofty seat, decided who was first on his legs. The parties then retired, a bell was rung, the curtain was raised at the end of the room, and the spouter or singer, making his bow, commenced his part. . . . The entertainment, as Lord Barrymore often said, was the most prolific of fun that his lordship, whose very being was to seek frolic, had ever witnessed in all his peregrinations. The night was waning fast, and we sat until exhilarated by copious draughts, and urged by his lordship, I yielded to my vanity, and undertook the part of Mother Cole, from Foote's celebrated farce of *The Minor*. . . . Lord Barrymore, entering heartily into the mirth which surrounded us, obeyed the general call for a song, a speech, or a recitation, and gave them a convivial strain with great glee.

A similar kind of evening entertainment, but on an entirely different level, was the Pic-Nic Society, which met at the Tottenham Rooms off Tottenham Court Road. This was a group of members of the nobility who, like the members of the Jacob's Well club, were stage-struck. They gave dramatic performances, accompanied by their own amateur orchestra, and drew such audiences that Drury Lane and Covent Garden began to be alarmed at this poaching.

The founder and leader was a Lady Albina Buckinghamshire, and the assemblies (on non-dramatic nights) were a sort of bottle-party. That is, the supper, or collation, and the wines were not bought by a committee and charged in the subscription. They were, as the name Pic-Nic suggested, contributed by the members, some sending game and meats, some sending pastries, fruit, wines, etc., at discretion. But the membership was large; Angelo says that "the Christmas larder at the famed Bush Inn, at Bristol, would scarcely suffice to furnish forth a single supper for these polite gourmands." And some of the members were very discreet in their contributions. So her ladyship ordered that lots should be drawn. A bag was provided in which were a number of labels inscribed with the name of some article for the supper-table, and a number of blanks.

The drawing of these lots afforded the town much amusement. It worked as matters of hazard usually do. Those with restricted means drew tickets for the most expensive things, and the very rich drew tickets for some trifle. The poor patrician drew a ticket for a Perigord pie, costing about three guineas, while the Duchess, whose Duke owned half a county, drew for a plum cake costing half-a-crown. A younger son would find in his fingers a label for a dozen of champagne, while the fifty-thousand-a-year baronet had drawn a ticket for a dozen oranges.

The Society was, as Angelo says, harmless, even rational, considering the general diversions of the fashionable world of that time; but the cartoonists and lampoonists got hold of it and laughed it off the scene. Certainly it gave them good material. Even Angelo himself, who was a member, and took part in the dramatic performances, has a laugh at their orchestra:

> Here, some descendant from the great and mighty baron of old, instead of being cased in armour, drew forth the fiddle-case; and he whose redoubtable ancestor wielded the battle axe at Cressy, here figured with the long-bow on a larger fiddle still; whilst one whose blood flowed through his thrice-noble veins, transmitted from the days of the Conqueror, conquered all hearts by his soft strains upon the flageolet. Here, too, quoting the audacious caricaturist, a giant lord warbled on the tiny flute, and a tiny lordling thundered on the double-bass. The gorgeous Lady Albina's dimpled fingers pressed the ivory keys of the grand piano, and Lady S . . . delighted the patrician auditory with a flourish on the French Horn.

Private theatricals were then a popular pastime among the well-to-do, and those of the Pic-Nic Society were serious and well-conducted. Private theatricals of a very different kind were those arranged at Wargrave, in Berkshire, by Lord Barrymore and his two brothers—known as Hell-gate, New-gate, and Cripple-gate; the first because of his manners, the second because he had been in prison, and the third because of a club-foot. The performances were indeed midnight revelries rather than serious dramatic shows. Lord Barrymore was inclined to fancy himself as a comic actor, and his house was always filled with a company of poets, actors, singers, and raconteurs whom he had picked up in the London taverns. He had a theatre built on to his house, and with this company, and himself and his brothers, he put on comedies and farces, and invited the neighbouring gentry as audience. The plays were given after dinner, usually about nine o'clock, and most of the cast were well pickled before they began. The fun was kept up all night, and bedtime at that house was often at sunrise.

Angelo says of him that all the pranks of Rochester, Ogle, the Duke of Buckingham, and others of the Restoration time were far outdone by him and his brothers. One of the noble lord's favourite amusements, after a late night in town, was to drive down to Wargrave in his phaeton, which was unusually high, and on passing through a village or town to slash right and left with his whip at the dark windows of the houses and crack them. Another was to go to Vauxhall, and start a riot. Riots at the Gardens were scarcely ever started by the common people or the citizens; almost always some titled blackguard was behind them, such as this Barrymore. There was one night when he hired a professional bruiser, dressed him as a clergyman, and ordered the waiters to let him have as much drink as he wanted. The result, of course, was a fighting parson. After a Vauxhall night, instead of going home he would drive to the Star and Garter at Richmond for breakfast, or row down-river and take the Margate Hoy. Reckless, mindless, and dissolute, he died at the age of twenty-four. A loaded gun in his curricle slipped from the seat on which he had placed it, and he received the full charge in his head.

Unusual entertainment was then as sure a draw to the bored and witless fashionables as it is to-day. Among the regular purveyors of evening pastime, invention was not very lively, so that when an amateur produced a novelty he was pretty sure of success. In the last quarter of the century two amateurs drew "all London" with exhibitions whose only claim to notice was that they were something new—like those lectures on Plato which some years ago Emil Reich delivered at a smart hotel to crowded audiences of excited women who can have had little idea what he was talking about. "Science" in the eighteenth century was as much a mumbo-jumbo word as it is to-day, and the shows which two scientific quacks imposed on the Almack world could have had no meaning at all for the silly heads that gaped at them. That didn't matter. They were new and they were sensational, and the quacks did very well with them.

One of them bore the rather sinister name of Dr. de Manneduke—no doubt an added attraction. His line was hypnotism. At his house in Bloomsbury he gave Sunday evening parties (at a price) and his drawing-rooms were crowded with the leaders of *ton* submitting themselves to pitiful exhibitionism. The "doctor" would approach each guest, make a few passes, and give an order; and here a girl would be shrieking with laughter, there a dowager fetching deep sighs and groans; elsewhere one would be fainting, another weeping pints of tears, another sitting rigid with the staring eyes of catalepsy.

Even more successful was the other quack, "Doctor" Graham, who ran a Temple of Health; a term which a doctor could use to embrace all manner of thrilling matter. He first caught his fashionable victims with the bait that always draws them—magnificently furnished rooms; and having got them, he kept them there with his lectures on The Female —with a half-clad model, named the Goddess of Health, who was later Lady Hamilton. Those evening lectures were apparently of such a nature that while female fashion flocked to them they were ashamed of having it known; they wore masks. Another of his lures which captured the Town was his lecture on the value of Earth-Bathing. In the middle of the lecture-room was a small pit half full of earth in which a chair was set. The doctor, half-clothed, would enter this pit and seat himself on the chair, when two lackeys would shovel more earth into the pit. As the earth rose about him, he would pull his shirt higher and higher, until the earth had reached his chest, and then would take the shirt right off, and the earth would be piled up to his neck. Then, sitting naked in this bath of earth, as he explained to his elegant audience, he would lecture on the virtues of mother earth, and what it did to the pores of the skin, and how it stimulated the blood.

Another of his lures had an even more intimate appeal. In a richly-furnished room he set up what he called his Celestial Bed. The Age of Reason was not very old, and had scarcely had time to exert much influence, even if reason had any hope of penetrating the world of fashion. The Celestial Bed was therefore an immediate success. It is not clear what made it Celestial, but the doctor's story was that it had valuable properties. It had been "charged" by certain ritual and ceremonial in such a way that it would rectify such physical impediments as impotence and sterility. So the Celestial Bed had quite a part in the night-life of certain circles; Angelo says that a childless Duke (unnamed) paid the required fee—five hundred guineas—for just one night's hire of it.

Just before the beginning of this present war, public poetry-reading was having quite a vogue. It was even being done in the village inn and the four-ale bars of the towns. It was, of course, nothing new; it was a revival of an evening entertainment which began in the later years of Dr. Johnson. Not that he took part in it; his delivery, one gathers from Boswell, did not add anything of grace to any lines or lyrics he might quote. But Thomas Sheridan (R. B.'s father), of whose oratory Johnson had a poor opinion, often gave readings, and for a time successfully. He employed the pompous declamatory manner, and usually limited himself to heroic verse.

There is a story which would have amused Johnson (he had died a few months earlier) of Sheridan doing a joint recital with Henderson, a well-known actor of the time. They took the Freemason's Hall in Great Queen Street, and filled it for several nights. Sheridan did his usual heroic stuff, and Henderson did comic things, among them a ballad which two or three years before had gone all over England—*John Gilpin*. Each time Henderson went on to read, the audience sat up.

Each time Sheridan went on, the audience sat back, and shuffled its feet. Sheridan produced his reserve-piece, *Alexander's Feast*, which had never failed to move an audience, but he gave it each night *after* Henderson, and it was received with no excitement. The vain and querulous Sheridan was annoyed. Still, the entertainments were successful in the matter of receipts, and as Sheridan considered himself the senior partner of the venture he collected the receipts, and, in acknowledgment of Henderson's kind services, handed him a small percentage as a gratuity. Henderson, in blank surprise at such behaviour, waved it away and walked out. The offices of a mutual friend had to be engaged to bring home to Sheridan the fact that Henderson had an equal, if not the larger part in the success of the entertainment, and that the receipts should be equally shared. It took some time to make Sheridan see this; his first response being "My God! What! Dryden's Ode to be put in competition with Gilpin's trash? Impossible!" Later, with a bad grace, he paid up, but his resentment of Henderson's demand, like his resentment of Johnson's attitude to himself, lasted for ever; they were never friends again.

In the last quarter of the century a new evening diversion, or a new form of an old diversion, arrived—the circus, or, as it was then called, the equestrian display. Just before 1780 Philip Astley, a riding-master, opened his amphitheatre in Westminster Bridge Road, where he offered feats of horsemanship, rope-dancing, and acrobatics. In the course of years it changed the form of its entertainment many times, but always it was equestrian. It remained a feature of London's night-life until the 1860's, and it wrote its name into the story of entertainment as London's first—and last—permanent circus; "permanent" being allowed, I think, in the short-life world of entertainment, to a continuous season in one place through eighty years.

London still, for a capital, had few regular theatres. There were the two patent theatres, very jealous of their rights; the Haymarket theatre; the theatre at Goodman's Fields; Sadler's Wells; the Royalty, in Wellclose Square, Wapping, and the Lyceum. At all except the first three the entertainment was, necessarily, mixed. Some large towns of the provinces had their Theatre Royal, and many of the small towns had a minor theatre; minor meaning that, like most of the London theatres, it could not present Shakespeare (the monopoly of the patent theatres) or legitimate drama. Minor theatres could present only spectacle or farce, comic lectures, burlettas, or plays turned into equestrian performances by the introduction of a few horses. Dialogue could only be used in those theatres when accompanied by music, a restriction which was responsible for the birth of the original Melo-Drama. Some theatres, wishing to present plays, dodged the law by turning them into operettas. Thus, one theatre presented *The Beaux' Stratagem* set to music, with lively songs interspersed; another did *Macbeth* as a ballet and *As You Like It* as a pantomime.

When the Surrey Theatre at St. George's Fields (now St. George's Circus) was opened by Charles Dibdin in 1782, it was under these same restrictions, and it opened ostensibly as a rival to Astley, and only by degrees chanced a disguised play or two. It called itself the Royal Equestrian Philharmónic Academy—comprehensive enough for any kind of show—and it announced itself to the public in these terms:

> This and every evening will be exhibited at this place a most capital and extensive variety of equestrian exercises, where the docility, strength, sagacity, and gracefulness of that noble animal, the horse, will be evinced in a great number of striking instances, as well as the expertness, agility, and ease of the various performers, whose different manoeuvres and evolutions exceed description and cannot be equalled by any other collection in Europe. The lady from St. Sebastian will assist in the performances, and the whole of the horsemanship will be conducted under the immediate direction of that unparalleled horseman, Mr. Hughes. In relief to the horsemanship, and during the intermediate spaces allowed for the repose of the performers, will be given a species of amusement perfectly novel in its kind, consisting of paintings, statues, and heterogeneous objects, properly explained and elucidated, and brought into three parts under the following titles—*The Barrier of Parnassus*, *The Land of Enchantment*, and lastly, a grand Oriental spectacle with superb decorations, a procession of transparent figures, and a most brilliant display of fireworks, called *The Temple of Confucius*. Begins precisely at half-past six. A horse patrol is provided from bridge to bridge.

Towards the end of the century, night-life among certain groups in London, and in the provincial pleasure resorts, became wilder and sillier. Those groups drew their inspiration from Upper Circles; they were composed of those dull followers of fashion who watch what the Highly Placed are doing, and copy it. At that time the Highly Placed meant the Prince, who had just come of age and had been granted his own establishment, and was setting the pace in all kinds of nonsense and all those gaieties which, in Cowper's lines, "fill the bones with pain, the mouth with blasphemy, the heart with woe." Or rather, those around him were setting the pace, and he was content to let them. The shabbier kind of night-life of that turbulent period had as its core the sponging entourage of that untrained young man. They created no new diversion, nor did they follow the sensible diversions of their time. All they did was to repeat, on an extravagant scale, the amusements of the lout—practical jokes, tap-room humour, the boxing-ring, the racecourse, the card-table, and the brothel; according to some veiled reports the more unusual type of brothel; or, as Gronow puts it, "the profligate life led by his Royal Highness, and those admitted to his intimacy, was such as to make it a matter of wonder that such scandalous scenes of debauchery could be permitted in a country like ours."

But with this behaviour they set a fashion which was followed by many of their contemporaries of wealth and position, and which lasted till about the middle of the nineteenth century, and even took a name to itself—Corinthianism. It spread from Carlton House and the Brighton Pavilion all over England. Pastimes which had belonged to the mob became the pastimes of the aristocracy. It was the ambition of the younger nobility to be able to "mill" like a professional bruiser, to drive a mail-coach, and spit tobacco-juice, like a coachman, and to swear like a black-leg. There is a Sheridan anecdote which records his being asked by a noble lady: "Why, Mr. Sheridan, do our young men of birth persist in dressing, looking, and talking like boxers and grooms?" To which Sheridan answered: "I never had a turn for family secrets, madam, but I suspect *birth* to be the cause."

The Prince's circle at that time was composed of the Duke of Cumberland (his uncle) who had quarrelled with George III and led the son away in a sort of spite; Colonel George Hanger; Charles James Fox; R. B. Sheridan; and Lord Barrymore and his brother—Hellgate and Cripplegate. By this group he was easily transformed from a weak and aimless nothing into the First Rake of Europe. None of them could have been a good influence on a young man who had been kept uninstructed and under domestic restraint until he was eighteen; and the most dangerous influence (naturally) was not the cynical Fox, or the crude Hanger, or the half-mad Hellgate and Cripplegate, but the charming, brilliant, insouciant Sheridan, who was the very opposite of his industrious and respectable elocutionist father. In almost all the pranks and orgies recorded of the Prince in those early years, Sheridan had a leading part.

The Press and the cartoonists did not spare that coterie. The newspapers of that time were not afraid to expose scandalous behaviour among the great, or to express the public distaste; it is only under democracy that the Press has thrown "glamour" over the doings of very silly people. Cartoons of the period show the Prince being carried drunk from Brooks' club by Fox; they show him being married to Mrs. Fitzherbert, with the assistance of Fox, Hanger, and Sheridan; they show him drunk in the kitchens of the Brighton Pavilion; and they show him, at the time when his debts had become a national question and the king had refused to help him, sitting by a cottage fire with Mrs. Fitzherbert, roasting a sheep's-head for their dinner, with George Hanger bringing in a jug of beer.

The Press held the same tone. Serious criticism of his conduct was made by serious papers, and the others supplied facetious squibs and ballads. One of these, quoted by John Ashton in his *Florizel's Folly*, presents him as giving orders for departure to Brighton:

> The pockets of the coach well cram
> With brandy, gin, and carraway,
> That we may take a social dram
> When snugly riding far-away. . . .
>
> And we will sport and feast away,
> In one unbroken revel;
> Venus all night, and wine all day;
> We'll play the very devil.

The *Morning Post* in 1785 commented on the kind of company he drew to Brighton: "Brighthelmstone is at present very thin of company, few females arriving there but the *corps d'amour*. Women of virtue and character shun these scenes of debauchery and drunkenness, ever attendant on the spot which is the temporary residence of a P——." In 1788 it gave a sketch of the behaviour of the company:

> When the dinner hour arrives, after these sprightly and heroic gentlemen have slain their thousands and ten thousands, according to their own account, in the field . . . they then attire themselves in order to enjoy the pleasures of the table; and however deranged they may afterwards be by convivial excess, they march or stagger away to the Rooms, as circumstances may determine, and entertain the ladies with elegant and decent gallantry. . . . If a spectator, not cognizant in the fanciful and capricious variations of *ton*, were to cast his eyes on the motley group contained in the Rooms of an evening, far from supposing them persons of the first fashion attired for a ball, he would consider them as a band of Bedlamites; or at best conclude that the whole presented the extravagant vagaries of a masquerade.

A little later in the same year it paid him a compliment, if a left-handed one: "The Prince gains many hearts by his great affability and good humour. His company is much better than it used to be, and he is certainly more sparing of his libations to Bacchus. . . . The Prince has won money on the races—more money than one would wish a Prince of Wales to win."

The story of the trick he played on the gluttonous and bibulous old Duke of Norfolk of that time—"Jockey" Norfolk—is familiar to most readers, but it makes a contrast to another picture of Pavilion nights, when he was showing his more sensible and agreeable self. "Jockey" Norfolk was known as a man who could drink from noon to the following dawn without collapsing. In those days when hard drinking was general, he would be one of a party of hard drinkers at a St. James Street tavern, and would drink bottle for bottle with them, and see them severally disappear under the table. Then he would go to one of the clubs, and join a new convivial party, and see *them* out. At the Beef Steak Club he would consume five rump steaks at a sitting, and several bottles of port, having previously taken, by way of appetiser, a small fish course at some tavern on the way—probably about half a turbot.

On this particular occasion the Prince determined to get him drunk for the fun of seeing how he would behave. He was invited to the Pavilion to dine and sleep, and every member of the company was ordered to invite him to take wine. He arrived from Arundel, and at the dinner he was pledged again and again. The pledging was so constant that he began to scent something; but he held out well, and saw several of the company overcome. When he had taken enough to have put out three ordinary men, he was still sitting. The Prince then pledged him in a bumper of brandy, but waited for the duke to drink first. The duke rose and emptied the bumper, and then asked the royal permission to ring for his carriage and go home. The Prince reminded him that he had come to dine and sleep. He answered that the treatment he had received gave him no desire to enjoy such an honour; he had been brought there to make sport. He would have no more of it. He once more asked for his carriage, and said that he would never again enter a house where he had been so treated.

The Prince gave orders for the carriage to be brought round. There was some delay in horsing it and getting it round, and by the time it arrived the last bumper had done its work. The Duke was asleep. The Prince roused him, and he got somehow out of the banqueting-room and to the door. He fell into the carriage and ordered the postilions to drive Home. When he was in, the Prince countermanded the order, and he and such of his party as could still stand stood in the drive and watched Norfolk being driven round and round the lawn for about half an hour. When the carriage at last pulled up they lifted Norfolk out asleep, and he woke next morning in the house he had determined never again to enter.

The other side of the Prince is shown in an account of life at the Pavilion when he had his Princess (Caroline) and his young daughter Charlotte with him. He seems to have spent much time in showing his daughter on this first visit all the delights of his monstrous gilded toy. No Court etiquette was observed until the six o'clock dinner, at which all the company assembled. After dinner other guests arrived, and there was music and cards, or the guests could stroll about from room to room, the Prince moving among them and talking "with the most affable condescension." At half-past eleven their Royal Highnesses retired, and the evening closed.

There is another little story showing his good-nature when he was out of the influence of the stupid company that gathered round and toadied to him. Somebody—probably one of that stupid company—thought of what he would have called "a prime bit of gig" which would give everybody a laugh. To a quiet and obscure attorney, who was taking a holiday at Brighton with his wife, he sent a forged invitation to an evening reception at the Pavilion. The attorney and his wife, warm and wondering at the honour of being noticed, duly arrived, and were escorted to the great Saloon where half the nobility was already assembled, not one of whom they knew. After standing for some time in awkward isolation, while the Prince received his guests, they were at last led up and their names announced.

He had a royal memory for people, and in one glance he knew that the couple were strangers to him, and that no invitation had been sent to anybody of their name. He asked questions. The attorney produced his invitation. The Prince saw at once that some trick had been played upon them, and with admirable social dexterity he rescued them from their dilemma. Some merry wag, he said, had no doubt done this with the intention of sporting with their feelings, but for himself, he felt indebted to this wag since it had given him the pleasure of making their acquaintance, and he was sincerely happy in this opportunity of receiving them. During the rest of the evening he went out of his way to talk to them, to present them to others of the company, and to pay them a number of little attentions which set them entirely at their ease, and gave him two loyal subjects who for the rest of their lives would never hear a word against him.

When he was not *en famille*, his nights were spent either with his boon companions, the Lads of the Fancy, or with company of a quite different sort. Like a true prince, he could be all things to all men, but his two strongest inclinations were towards gross bottle company, on the one side, or the company of men of distinguished abilities, on the other. Anybody who saw him at Carlton House or the Pavilion in one of those characters could hardly believe the stories of the other. His favour went always to men who could amuse him in either an intelligent way or an uproarious way. He had a sincere appreciation of the arts and a real love of letters and of wit. Music was one of his interests, and at London and Brighton many musical evenings were arranged in which he took part both with violin and voice—though his voice, a basso, had little quality beyond volume. Gronow mentions a captain of the Royal Artillery who received a peerage, not for services to the state but for his merits in accompanying his royal master in the 'cello part of a string quartet.

The Prince was an example of the men of his time; gamesters, drunkards, haunters of the lowest dens, careering about the streets at midnight smashing windows; and having with it all a number of accomplishments, informed minds, sound scholarship, and taste in literature. A sketch of Lord Barrymore might serve as a sketch of his patron and of all the others: "Alternately between the gentleman and the blackguard, the refined wit and the most vulgar bully were equally well known in St. James's and St. Giles's. He could fence, dance, drive, or drink, box or bet with any man in the kingdom. He could discourse slang as trippingly as French, relish porter after port, and compliment her ladyship at a ball with as much ease and brilliance as he could bespatter in a cider cellar."

And though the Prince, when, in 1811, he became Regent, changed his entourage and calmed his ways, the Corinthianism which he had encouraged was maintained and carried over from the 1700's to the 1800's. So that the night life of the Regency period and of George's kingship was, by that small but vociferous and widely-scattered section, made more boisterous than at any time before or since. There are many witnesses to the fact that four-bottle men often joined the ladies in the drawing-room in a state which in later years would have emptied the room; and in most public assemblies, except Almack's, which perhaps could hardly be called public, there was a display of free manners and loud remark and bold stare which belonged to the Roderick Random age. The years were the years of the nineteenth century, but the tone was still of the middle Hanoverian age. I have maintained elsewhere that no given century can be taken as a figure to express a particular way of life in manners, customs, and modes. We live by ages, and these ages form themselves at odd times. The temper and accent of those ages cannot be caught by setting a rigid period beginning with the first year of a century and ending at its hundredth. The nineteenth century has become synonymous with respectability and gigmanity. It could not therefore have begun with 1801, which led on to the rowdy 1820's. It did not, in fact, begin till 1837.

35 A Ballet at the Opera House
From the Rowlandson and Pugin print of 1809

36 Astley's Amphitheatre
From the Rowlandson and Pugin print of 1809

37 The Waltz

We won't go Home till Morning

Then, dress, then dinner, then awakes the world;
Then glare the lamps, then whirl the wheels, then roar
Through street and square fast flashing chariots, hurled
Like harnessed meteors.

BYRON

LONDON NIGHT-LIFE in the first quarter of the 1800's was various both in its diversions and in the quality of those diversions. There were the formal and elegant nights of Holland House and Almack's; the more formal but less elegant nights of Carlton House; the theatre and tavern and club nights; the opera nights; and those nights at certain smart and notorious houses, which many of the male nobility attended, and of which we can get an idea from Harriette Wilson's account of the receptions given at the house of her sister Amy.

Table customs in London continued to be those of the country. In the country, where there was nothing else to do, there was some excuse for the long-strung parade of dishes and the procession of wines; but in London and other cities, which offered variety of entertainment, surely nothing but gluttony could have kept men eight hours at table. Angelo records a supper he attended at the Thatched House Tavern, given by the royal Duke of Sussex in 1806. The Prince was the chief guest. They sat down at nine o'clock. The solid part of the supper, the eating, went on till about one in the morning, the Duke seeing that glasses were re-filled every five minutes. Angelo stuck to one wine (hock), and to this he attributed the fact that he was able to keep his head. At one o'clock the cloth was drawn, and the decanters set on the table, and the serious part of the drinking began. Songs were called for. The Prince obliged with a song. Tom Moore obliged. Other guests obliged. When songs began to pall, the Duke introduced on to the table a dwarf, who danced among the decanters and dessert. Fresh wines were introduced to whet the palate, and more songs were given. The company rose from table at five o'clock.

Formal dinners of that kind might consist of only a few courses, but each course had many dishes, and it was the custom to taste "something of everything." One dinner of that time, for a company of fifteen, may be taken as typical of many:

Turtle Soup

Turtle Cutlets
Whitebait
Sauté of Haddock
Turbot
Fillets of Whitings
John Dory

Boiled Chickens
Roast Chickens
Ham Tongue

Tendrons of Lamb

Haunch of Venison

Larded Poults
Roast Goose
Roast Hare
Roast Quails
Salade Italienne

Tart
Jelly
Cheese-cakes
Cabinet Pudding
Prawns

With that dinner went Madeira, Champagne, Hermitage, Burgundy, Bordeaux (22 bottles), Hock, and Port. Gronow's description of the dinners of that time was that they were solid, hot, and stimulating. "The dessert, if for a dozen people, would cost at least as many pounds. . . . A perpetual thirst seemed to come over people, both men and women, as soon as they had tasted their soup; as from that moment everybody was taking wine with everybody else till the close of the dinner; and such wine as produced that class of cordiality which frequently wanders into stupefaction. How all this sort of eating and drinking ended was obvious."

The social occasions of the middle and professional classes were conducted with a little more sense. The eccentric and at that time famous Dr. Kitchiner, author of *The Art of Cookery* and a treatise on music, gave excellent and well-devised dinners to his friends. He would invite them to attend his house at such-and-such an hour to join a Committee of Taste and Eta Beta Pie. He also, once a week, held conversazioni, where all the lively and intelligent spirits of the time were seen. The entertainment was talk, music and song, or perhaps a visit to his roof-observatory, where he had a telescope and studied astronomy. But for both dinners and conversazioni he had one strict rule, which was printed and fixed above the mantel-shelf—*Come at Seven. Go at Eleven.* Since few parties get warmed up before the third hour, it meant that his guests often had to break-up in mid-air of their interest and merriment. Their reluctance at observing this rule was once hinted by the younger George Colman. He made a slight alteration in the notice, adding one word, so that it read—*Come at Seven. Go It at Eleven.* The good doctor ignored the hint, and closing time remained as it was. At the break-up of each dinner-party his guests were offered in the hall a stirrup-cup, intended to correct any ill-effects of the dinner and the wines. They were offered a glass of camomile tea; a rather chilling farewell to those who were in the mood expressed by the convivial lyrist:

> A bumper at parting, a bumper so bright,
> Though the clock points to morning, by way of good-night.
> Time, scandal, and cards are for tea-drinking souls,
> Let them play their rubbers, while we ply the bowls.
> Oh, who are so jocund, so happy as we?
> Our skins full of wine, and our hearts full of glee.

The parties and receptions given by Harriette Wilson's sister Amy were equally discreet in tone, though they usually began when the doctor's were done, and ended at dawn. Harriette and her three sisters, Amy, Fanny, and Sophia, four of the best known Cyprians of their time, were the daughters of a man named Debouchet, a clock-maker, said to be the offspring of a union between the Earl of Chesterfield and a Continental *limonadière*. The mother, a maker of silk stockings, was also illegitimate. According to Charles Westmacott, a notorious slanderer, the mother brought the girls up to her own business, and used to set them to work in the parlour window, where their attractions could be observed by the dashing young men of *ton*. In other words, he says she offered them to the world.

Amy, the eldest, passed as Amy Sydenham; Harriette as the name by which she is best known. Both had a career among the more gallant nobility, but neither finished in its ranks. Amy in her middle age married a harpist named Bochsa, and Harriette a half-pay officer named Rochforte. By her own account, given in the opening sentence of her *Memoirs*, Harriette became the mistress of the Earl of Craven at the age of fifteen, and lived thereafter under the protection of many great names. Amy also lived under various protectors, and in the intervals distributed her favours here and there. Fanny lived mostly under the protection of Lord Hertford—Thackeray's "Marquis of Steyne." Sophia, the youngest, the hard-boiled simpleton of the family, did better than any of them. When she was thirteen she was seduced by a nasty Lord Deerhurst, and a year or two later she retired from the fray as a Duchess. She caught the eye of the Duke of Berwick, and by her bland and child-like docility lured him, without trying or wanting, into a serious and legal marriage.

None of those girls could be called beautiful or even pretty, but they had attractions and accomplishments, vivacity and espièglerie, which set them in the aristocracy of their profession. Amy was an agreeable musician, and spoke and read French, Italian, and Spanish. Harriette herself, from a contemporary picture, was remarkably plain, but she was a witty talker, and had a "way" with her. Sophia's chief point was her childish charm; otherwise, from her sister's account of her, she was what we now call "dumb," though, like most of the "dumb," able to get all sorts of things that others strove in vain for. The most pleasant of the four, in character and temperament, was Fanny; she was sensible and gentle, and of goodwill. Plain as they were, each of these sisters was pursued by members of the peerage. Amy's house was a nightly rendezvous for the most distinguished males, and she and Harriette disposed of their favours at their own price. Harriette could command a hundred guineas for a few hours of her company. None of their admirers ventured to take any liberty with them. They were not women of the town. Though they had no place in the great world, they were princesses of the half-world, and often their company was sought merely for its own bright sake.

Harriette describes one of the nights at Amy's, where, she says, all the world was present, and not room enough for them:

> Some were in the passage, and some in the parlour, and in the drawing-room one could scarcely breathe. At the top of it Amy sat coquetting with her tall Russian. The poor Count Palmella stood gazing on her at a humble distance.

The company included George Brummell, Count Benckendorff, Henry Luttrell, Lord Alvanley, Lord Palmerston, and the Hon. George Ward, later Earl of Dudley. During supper, a buffet-supper, George Ward was for some reason made the butt of the company:

> Brummell, in his zeal for cold chicken, soon appeared to forget everybody in the room. A loud discordant laugh from the Honourable John Ward, who was addressing something to Luttrell at the other end of the table, led me to understand that he had just, in his own opinion, said a very good thing; yet I saw his corner of the room full of serious faces.
> "Do you keep a valet, sir?" said I.
> "I believe I have a rascal of that kind at home," said the learned ugly scion of nobility with disgusting affectation.

"Then," I retorted, "do, in God's name, bring him next Saturday to stand behind your chair."

"For what, I pray?"

"Merely to laugh at your jokes," I rejoined. "It is such hard work for you, sir, who have both to cut the jokes and to laugh at them too!"

"Do pray show him up, there's a dear creature, whenever you have an opportunity," whispered Brummell in my ear, with his mouth full of chicken. "Is he not an odious little monster of ill-nature, take him altogether?" I asked. "And look at that tie!" said Brummell, shrugging up his shoulders, and fixing his eyes on Ward's neckcloth.

Ward was so frightened at this commencement of hostilities from me that he immediately began to pay his court to me, and engaged me to take a drive with him the next morning in his curricle.

Another *petit souper* which she describes was given by one of her admirers at his hotel in Dover Street, and was not so decorous. The other guests were the Hon. George Lamb, the host's mistress, and the always-drunk Elliston of Drury Lane. They went first to the theatre, to see Elliston in a new piece, and when the show was over he joined them in the coach of their host. But the coachman was too drunk to drive, and so drunk that he indignantly refused to surrender the reins to the footman. Elliston jumped out of the coach, and said he would deal with the fellow. George Lamb expressed a fear that Elliston might attempt to drive them home himself; he could bear anything but that. But Elliston only got on the box and "quietly threw the drunken coachman off on to the pavement, box-coat and all, in spite of his swearing and kicking." The host jumped out of the coach, and picked his coachman up, to see if he was alive, and then somebody called the watch. The watch came, and after some moments of turmoil Elliston got back into the coach and ordered the footman to drive to Dover Street. One of the company asked where the host was, and Elliston's airy answer was that he had been taken to the watch-house.

When they arrived at Dover Street, Elliston took charge of affairs. They found an "elegant" supper laid out, with plenty of champagne. Elliston explained to the host's servant that his master had gone to the watch-house and had requested himself to do the honours. They sat down to supper without the host, and Elliston got more and more drunk. When the host at last arrived, Elliston joined him in rehearsing a song in a new light piece, and, knowing only the first line of the song, sang it as "Oh, 'tis love, 'tis love, 'tis love, 'tis love, 'tis love. . . ."

"Elliston," bawled out George Lamb, "why the deuce don't you come and finish your supper? I want to speak to you."

Elliston took no notice, but continued his "Oh, 'tis love, 'tis love, 'tis love!"

"Livius, then," said George Lamb, "I want to ask you whether you have places to spare for your night."

"Elliston won't allow me to leave off," replied Livius, still continuing to play to Elliston's "Oh, 'tis love, 'tis love, 'tis love!"

"Leave off, you blockhead," said George Lamb to Elliston. "I will lay you fifty guineas that you do not repeat one line as Livius has written it, either in your song or your speech."

Elliston appeared to agree, and give up the matter as hopeless, for, darting from the pianoforte towards Livius's young female friend, who still continued at table, he gave her such an ardent embrace that she was quite frightened, and then, as I sat next, he conferred the same honour on me. "Good heavens, what a mountebank is here," said I, pushing him from me. George Lamb sat next, for he had not half finished his supper. Elliston placed himself in a theatrical attitude, ready to embrace him. "And as to you, my George!" said he with much pathos. "For God's sake," exclaimed George Lamb, with his mouth full of dried cherries, "do not play the fool with me."

Harriette being what she was, her memoirs naturally are mostly concerned with the night hours. When early morning is mentioned it is almost always as the anti-climax of a big night, such as the midnight masquerade given by the members of Watier's club to the nobility of England and their Cyprian friends. Harriette went as an Italian peasant-girl; her sister Fanny as a country housemaid; and Amy exhibited her taste by going as a nun. Supper was served to over a thousand guests, and since it was directed by Watier, the royal chef, and prepared by Labourie, the famous head cook of the club, it was composed of materials from all over Europe, and was such a supper as those guests who were not members of the club seldom saw. After supper dancing was resumed until eight o'clock, when breakfast, with coffee, tea, and chocolate, was served. The party broke up at half-past nine.

After such metropolitan assemblies, the attempts at night-life which she experienced in the country could hardly have had much appeal. Her description of Lyme Regis presents an odd picture to those who know it in present times:

> Lyme Regis is a sort of Brighton in miniature, all bustle and confusion, assembly-rooms, donkey-riding, raffling, etc. It was sixpence per night to attend the assemblies, and much cheaper if paid by the season. . . . From the window I was much amused to see the number of smart old maids that were tripping down the streets, in turbans or artificial flowers twined around their wigs, on the light fantastic toe, to the sixpenny assembly rooms. They were very pleasantly situated, near the sea, and as we walked past their windows, we saw them all drinking tea and playing at cards. There were, amongst them, persons of the highest rank. . . .

Night-life in the hunting country was even duller. At Melton Mowbray, where she was a nightly guest of the men's dinner club, the evening was spent at the table, and broke up at ten with the company half asleep. The only diversion was that caused by the local frail ones, who paraded outside the club windows, or stood looking in and tapping to attract attention. But at Falmouth she found things a little livelier, and was able, with the help of the navy, to go to the play, and then to dance and sup till three in the morning.

One of her host of friends was Tom Sheridan, who had acquired most of his father's bad habits, and some share of his wit if not of his genius. He had from so early an age turned night into day that even in his twenties he was showing signs of physical wreckage, and it was a little surprising that he lived to reach the age of forty-two. There is an anecdote turning on father and son at supper on an occasion when Tom, even so late in the day, was still suffering from the night before, and was all starts and jumps. During supper, the servant attending them knocked over the plate-warmer and sent two dozen plates crashing to the floor, which set Tom shivering and quaking. "Clumsy fool," said Sheridan senior. "Smashed the whole lot, I suppose?"

"No, sir," said the servant, brightly; "not one."

"Not one! Damme, d'ye mean to say you've made all that noise for nothing!"

Among the mass of Sheridaniana is a story of his being found in the street by the watch so drunk that he couldn't stand and could scarcely speak. As he was well dressed they asked him where he wanted to go. He didn't know. They asked him where he lived. He couldn't remember. "Well, what's your name?" That question he managed to answer. Out it came—"Wilberforce!"

Byron, in one of his letters to Moore, describes a typical Sheridan evening:

> Yesterday I dined out with a large-ish party, where were Sheridan and Colman, Harry Harris, of C. G. and his brother, Sir Gilbert Heathcote, and others of note and notoriety. Like other parties of the kind, it was first silent, then talky, then argumentative, then disputatious, then unintelligible, then altogethery, then inarticulate, and then drunk. When we had reached the last step of this glorious ladder, it was difficult to get down again without stumbling; and to crown all Kinnaird and I had to conduct Sheridan down a damned corkscrew staircase, which had certainly been constructed before the discovery of fermented liquors, and to which no legs, however crooked, could possibly accommodate themselves. We deposited him safe at home, where his man, evidently used to the business, waited to receive him in the hall. Both he and Colman were, as usual, very good, but I carried away much wine, and the wine had previously carried away my memory; so that all was hiccough and happiness for the last hour or so, and I am not impregnated with any of the conversation. . . . My paper is full, and I have a grievous headache.

A little different from an evening party which happened about the same time, though in a novel—Mr. Woodhouse's party in *Emma*. It presents a useful companion-piece, since it was typical of many parties in many houses of that England; the quiet, middle-class party which seldom got recorded because it threw up nothing but pleasant intercourse between friends. If you don't remember Mr. Woodhouse's morning-after reflections, here they are:

> "I hope everybody had a pleasant evening," said Mr. Woodhouse, in his quiet way. "I had. Once, I felt the fire rather too much; but then I moved back my chair a little, a very little, and it did not disturb me."

As a pendant to Byron's evening with Sheridan, Moore, in his *Life of Byron*, records one or two evenings with his subject. On one of these he had invited Byron to supper, and, knowing that Byron had eaten nothing for some days beyond biscuits, he had ordered a fish supper. Byron considered the fish, but would touch nothing but lobsters. Hardly a thing with which to break a long fast, but he ate three. With them he took small glasses of old white brandy, and an occasional glass of hot water; six glasses of brandy to two or three of water. This was followed by claret, a bottle each, and they broke up at about four in the morning. This, according to Moore, was a fairly regular procedure with Byron when he supped. He speaks of other nights which he had the happiness of passing with Byron; of a night when, on the way home from some late assembly, they passed Stevens's Hotel in Bond Street, and saw the lights still burning. Byron suggested supper, and they went in, and the supper was again lobsters and white brandy, and they broke up in broad daylight.

Club-life was not at that time so much a part of all men's nights as it became some twenty years later. The big clubs with their own premises did not then fill both sides of Pall Mall. The clubs that existed in that street and St. James' Street were mainly political, or only for men of rank and property, and their chief feature was the gaming-room. White's, Brooks', Arthur's, Boodle's, and Watier's were the existing clubs, and stories are told in connection with all of them of parties sitting at the hazard table through a night, the whole of the next day, the following night, and up to noon of the second day, tiring out three shifts of waiters. Often, at the end of a sitting, fifty thousand pounds had changed hands or gone into the bank. At some clubs the players wore a special costume. To save damage to their fine clothes they put on frieze coats and a sort of leather mitten to protect their cuffs. As a

38 Brooks's Club, *ca.* 1800
From a drawing by Thomas Rowlandson

39 Episodes in the Life of a Regency Buck
From a print by Henry Alken

40 The Bruisers and the Ladies
From a print by Thomas Rowlandson

41 The Dram Shop, 1816
From a plate by Thomas Rowlandson

protection against the glare of light, they also wore broad-brimmed straw hats, and, to prevent opponents from guessing by their expressions what sort of cards they were backing, the hats were fitted with tassels which hung before the eyes.

The professional men continued to spend their evenings in little coteries at the taverns, and many men of the peerage, who did not care for gaming or for the promiscuity of club-life, would spend their evenings and meet their particular friends at one of the hotels that were then a new feature of the London scene. According to Gronow, the hotels these fastidious men patronised were Grillon's, in Albemarle Street; Limmer's, the Clarendon, Long's, Stevens', all in Bond Street; Fladong's, in Oxford Street; and Ibbetson's. The Clarendon, he says, was the only public place where a real French dinner was served. The price was between three and four pounds, and a bottle of champagne, or even Bordeaux, was a guinea. They were not, all of them, places of any magnificence, but in those days men of taste often had queer taste, and a lord who would flout White's would carry his fastidiousness to some quite common establishment. Gronow describes Limmer's as:

> A midnight Tattersall's, where you heard nothing but the language of the turf, and where men with not very clean hands used to make up their books. Limmer's was the most dirty hotel in London; but in the gloomy, comfortless coffee-room might be seen many members of the rich squirearchy who visited London during the sporting season. This hotel was frequently so crowded that a bed could not be obtained for any amount of money; but you could always get a very good plain English dinner, an excellent bottle of port, and some famous gin-punch.

Fladong's was a centre for the navy; Ibbetson's for the clergy and University men; Stevens's for military men. Gronow says of Stevens's that if any stranger went there for dinner, the servants merely looked at him and told him that all tables were engaged. The only dishes it served were boiled fish, fried soles, and joints.

Almack's continued to be the general rendezvous for the pick—and only the pick—of the top drawer. Its existence caused heart-burning among men as well as women. To be a member of White's was something, but it counted for little against receiving a card for Almack's assemblies and balls. About the time of Waterloo, the ladies' committee, which scrutinised and passed, or rejected, applications for the men's tickets, was composed of Lady Castlereagh, Lady Jersey, Lady Cowper, Lady Sefton, Princess Esterhazy, and the Countess Lieven.

All sorts of subterfuge and intrigue were used in attempts to influence a favourable decision from these ladies, some of whom, it was said, used their office to pay off scores against other women by refusing votes to their husbands. Many a man and woman, whose rank gave them admittance to the highest circles, went about hot with resentment against the arbitrary power exercised by the committee, when they had to answer the question—Would they be at Almack's to-morrow night? —with a No. One man, a captain of the Guards, learning that he had been excluded by the vote of the Countess of Jersey, sent a challenge to Lord Jersey, asking him to name his seconds and weapon. Lord Jersey's answer was that if every Guards officer who was blackballed by his wife were to call him out, he would be nothing but a constant target.

In addition to their rigid decisions as to who was and who was not presentable, the ladies ordained what costume the men should wear. One fixed rule was knee-breeches and white cravat, and when the Duke of Wellington arrived one night in trousers he was turned away. One point about these assemblies is a point one may note in the highest society of any time—the company was composed almost wholly of nobodies, people of no account to-day, and even in their own time, like the common people, unknown outside their immediate circle of friends.

It is a long drop from Almack's to the taverns of art and letters, but the company at least is as alive as any gathering of Lord Tom Noddies and tepid countesses, and much more piquant, even pungent. And the names have a significance which no longer attaches to dead nobility. There is nothing quite so dead as dead social figures, unless it be dead politicians. Ask your friends who was Home Secretary in 1893; who was Chancellor of the Exchequer in 1875; who was Secretary for War in 1858; who was Foreign Minister in 1884. And what offices were held by Mr. Childers, Mr. Bruce, and Mr. Lowe. I doubt if you would get correct answers. But the company to be found each night in the London taverns of the first quarter of the century would, if named, bring some response.

Rowlandson and Gillray were two of them. Henry Angelo mentions their meetings at the Coal Hole, in Fountain Court, off the Strand:

> For years he occasionally smoked his pipe at the Coal Hole or the Coach and Horses; and although the convives whom he met at such dingy rendezvous knew that he was that Gillray who fabricated those comical cuts, the very moral of Farmer George and Boney-Party, or Billy Pitt and Black Charly, he never sought, like that low coxcomb Morland, to become king of the company. He neither exacted, nor were they inclined to pay him, any particular homage. In truth, with his associates, neighbouring shopkeepers and master manufacturers, he passed for no greater wit than his neighbours. Rowlandson, his ingenious compeer, and he, sometimes met. They would perhaps exchange half-a-dozen questions and answers upon the affairs of copper and aquafortis;

swear all the world was one vast masquerade; and then enter into the common chat of the room, smoke their cigars, drink their punch, and sometimes early, sometimes late, shake hands at the door—look up at the stars, say it is a frosty night, and depart, one for the Adelphi, the other to St. James's Street.

At the Coal Hole, which was kept by Rhodes, the Singing Collier, Edmund Kean, in a mood of what used to be called *nostalgie de la boue*, founded his Wolves' Club, for supper, song, and good fellowship. Prominent members were Jack Bannister, Oxberry, Elliston, Liston, Braham, and Dibdin. There he spent his midnight leisure and squandered his health and his genius. When drawing-rooms were waiting to receive him, he turned his back on them, and proudly took the chair at the Wolves, whose members he exhorted to have "a pride that ranked them with the courtier and a philosophy that put them with the peasant." It was composed almost wholly of men connected with the theatre, sixty or seventy in number; a fraternity of Choice Spirits, passing the night in harmony and losing in each other's society all their wrongs and worries. Similar haunts to which he turned after his Drury Lane labours were a house in Villiers Street, kept by a retired singer; and the well-known theatrical house, the Harp Tavern, just by the theatre. In both these places, concert and dramatic entertainments were given by the would-be's and the has-beens—songs, Shakespearian soliloquies, imitations of the actors of the day. Each member of the company was expected to do something, and did; and proceedings went on till dawn.

Fitzgerald Molloy, in his *Life of Edmund Kean*, mentions another and peculiar night diversion of this genius, son of a drunken and mentally afflicted suicide, and great-grandson of another suicide, Henry Carey, composer of *Sally in our Alley*. Sometimes, Molloy says, after leaving the theatre, or the tavern to which he had gone after the theatre, he would mount a favourite horse, and ride madly through the night, across London and out to the country. There he would go at a gallop, jumping toll-gates in highwayman fashion, yelled at by turnpike-keepers and coachmen and, in the grey dawn, sworn at by frightened shepherds and field-workers. Some time in the early morning he would turn up at his house in Clarges Street, smothered in dust and half dead.

But mostly he preferred to sit at the head of the table at some theatrical tavern, where his talk, his songs, his acid wit, his imitations, his impromptu delivery of famous dramatic scenes and speeches in that marvellous voice were just what the great world would have liked to have and seldom had. When he did, on a rare occasion, acecpt an invitation to a great house, he would sit in a moody reserve from which nothing, not even a succession of glasses, could move him. This was set down to the eccentricity of genius. It really sprang from his knowledge that these people wanted him only because he was successful and a famous figure; and that none of them had helped him, or would have received him, in the days of his starving struggling as a stroller. He preferred to give what he had in the way of good company to those of his own profession who would appreciate and understand. He never forgot those who *had* helped him—most of them obscure managers and actors who never rose to better things—and he kept his best for them. He got them engagements; he acted without fee for their benefit; and he gathered them into his midnight tavern sittings. In those midnight sittings he was most himself and most expansive. They had him to themselves, and they alone knew the real Edmund Kean, the light and the dark of him.

There is a story of his reluctantly accepting an invitation from a noble lord who, to make the party more agreeable to Kean, had also invited another actor, Oxberry. The guests at dinner sat waiting for the flashes of brilliance and the sombre eloquence they had heard about, but none came. Then, as the cloth was being removed, and decanters set on, Kean caught Oxberry's eye, and whispered to him. "I prefer a quiet glass with a friend like you to all their champagne—effervescent, like themselves. Let's go." In the stir of movement made by the servants, they slipped out of the room, and out of the house, and went off to the Coal Hole.

He treated Byron in the same way. Byron greatly admired him, and, noting the way his habits were leading him, was anxious to reclaim him; a laudable intent, though in this particular case rather like a straw trying to support a broken reed. After many attempts he at last got an acceptance of a dinner invitation from Kean. But when the night arrived, Kean remembered that he had another engagement, and tried to beg off. Byron said he had invited several distinguished men to meet him, and that he must come. Kean gave in, and went. He was silent throughout the dinner, finding the company not at all amusing, and at the first opportunity he slipped away. Amid the talk and banter, nobody saw him go. When Byron at last noted that he was not there, he rang the bell and asked what had happened to Mr. Kean. The answer was that Mr. Kean, on arriving, had ordered his carriage to wait, and had gone off. The engagement to which he had gone was to take the chair at Tom Cribb's saloon in Panton Street, where some friends of his struggling days were having a supper. When Byron heard that his dinner-table had been deserted in favour of the company at a bruiser's tavern, he never again spoke to Kean.

Haydon the painter was not much of a tavern man, but during his early years in London he and Wilkie seem to have enjoyed some good evenings. Both liked the theatre. Haydon's taste was for drama; Wilkie's for farce and pantomime, the more idiotic, the better. In the *Autobiography* Haydon sums up those evenings:

> Painting all day; then dining at the Old Slaughter Chop House; then going to the Academy until eight to fill up the evening; then going home to tea—that blessing of a studious man—talking over our respective exploits, what he had been doing, and what I had done, and then, frequently, to relieve our minds fatigued by their eight and twelve hours' work, giving vent to the most extraordinary absurdities. . . . Sometimes, lazily inclined after a good dinner, we have lounged about near Drury Lane or Covent Garden, hesitating whether to go in, and often have I (knowing first that there was nothing I wished to see) assumed a virtue I did not possess, and pretending moral superiority, preached to Wilkie on the weakness of not resisting such temptations for the sake of our art and our duty, and marched him off to his studies when he was longing to see Mother Goose.

For those who could not afford the theatre, and Haydon often couldn't, there was another entertainment—the lowest form of theatre—the Penny Gaff. These penny theatres were illegal, but they were to be found all over London. They catered mainly for boys and girls, and played, five or six times a night, the most blood-curdling and desperate dramas of love and murder. He and Wilkie visited one of them in the Covent Garden Piazza:

> We entered and slunk away in a corner; while waiting for the commencement of the show, in came all our student friends one after the other. We shouted out at each one as he arrived, and then popped our heads down in our corner again, much to the indignation of the chimney sweeps and vegetable boys who composed the audience, but at last we were discovered, and then we all joined in applauding the entertainment of "Pull Devil, Pull Baker," and at the end raised such a storm of applause, clapping our hands, stamping our feet, and shouting with all the power of a dozen pair of lungs, that to save our heads from the fury of the sweeps we had to run downstairs as if the devil indeed was trying to catch us. After this boisterous amusement, we retired to my rooms and drank tea, talking away on art, starting principles, arguing long and fiercely, and at midnight separating, to rest, rise and work again until the hour of dinner brought us once more together.

Nights at the theatre in the first quarter of that century were exciting nights. You never knew what would happen, what the audience would demand of the actors and actresses, or how often they would call for the manager and give him their orders. Audiences in those days did not, as now, humbly submit to whatever rules and regulations haughty managers might impose upon them. *They* made the rules. It was for the manager to please *them*; to put on the actors and actresses they wanted to see in the plays they chose, at such prices as they felt were reasonable. They considered—and rightly—that they paid the manager and the cast, and, as employers, were entitled to give their orders. Actors then were really "servants of the public." Those who go to the theatre in our own time, particularly the West End theatre, have to suffer a lot of bad acting from young men and women who are there by virtue of qualities unconnected with the theatre; and they suffer in silence. In the early nineteenth century, audiences were less lymphatic, and often they staged their own drama.

Actors and actresses of to-day who become petulant, and even issue writs, because a critic in his notice has dismissed their bad work in a curt phrase, should look up old records and learn what actors of that time—some of them great actors—had to put up with. Bad acting, like bad singing at La Scala, Milan, was punished on the spot with hoots and hisses, often with apples, oranges and sticks. Sometimes the criticism was so insistent that the manager would bring the offender forward, and he would humbly apologise and promise to do better next time.

Junius Booth was once on the stage half an evening, unable to act except in dumb show, and not even permitted to apologise. At different times a stage-hand would come forward with a banner—Pray Silence to Explain. Then—Mr. Booth Will Apologise. And finally—Can Englishmen Condemn Unheard? But the uproar continued, and showed that Englishmen could. And all this because of a purely private dispute between young Booth and the managements of Covent Garden and Drury Lane, each of whom claimed exclusive right to his services. When Kemble raised the prices at the new Covent Garden theatre, the result was the famous O.P. Riots, and he had to apologise and return to the usual prices. Macready had to apologise for appearing in a part that did not suit him. Many another actor had to demean himself with explanations or excuses, and the manager was constantly being called for, sometimes four or five times in an evening, and had to come.

Kean, even at the summit of his career, received more of this treatment than any actor of his time. On one occasion he had twice in an evening to humble himself and beseech a hearing because he had missed a performance for which he was advertised. When, in his mid-career, he was involved in an action for damages, brought by a City alderman on the ground of adultery with his wife, his next appearance at the theatre was greeted with such howls and execrations as stunned and bewildered him and gave him a wound from which he never recovered. The play was *Richard III* but nobody heard it. His appearance so soon after the trial was taken as an insult to public morals, and the theatre was filled with hoots, howls, and groans. Oranges and orange-peel were flung at him, some of which struck him. Act by act he went through the play, while the tumult continued, and free fights went on in different parts of the house. Four times he came forward to address them, but could get not a moment of silence. From all sides foul names were hurled at him, and the night ended in riot.

Four days later he appeared as Othello, and was greeted by a similar tempest of execration. Elliston was then manager, and twice tried to get a hearing. He did not succeed until the middle of the after-piece, when he explained that he had engaged Mr. Kean before the action, and had announced the engagement for those dates, and had had bills printed. He could not break the engagement. He then begged the audience to hear Mr. Kean, and brought him forward; and the greatest tragedian of his age, while he did not apologise for the conduct of his private life, did stand before them, bent and subdued, and throw himself on their mercy. "If the public is of opinion that my conduct merits exclusion from the stage, I am ready to bow to its decision, and take my farewell." And all because he had been entangled by a scheming woman and her compliant husband. One can hardly see a leading actor of these days, who has been through the divorce court, either receiving that treatment from an audience, or bowing to it. Though many of us, I think, would like one or two of our "West End actors" to be given a little Edmund Kean treatment.

Some time later, when the worry and persecution arising from that case had deranged his volatile mind, he was to appear as Henry V. In scene after scene he found that he had completely lost his lines. He muffed them, dropped them, gagged, and was constantly moving to the wings for the prompter's help. He was greeted by hoots and hisses and calls for the manager. In the last act Kean stepped forward to make an apology. He explained that he had worked hard for their entertainment; that he had suffered privations when young, and that his constant labour since then had put a great strain upon him; that it was painful to him to incur the displeasure of those who had once given him approbation; that he appealed to their liberality as Englishmen. . . . But the only response he got were cries reminding him that he had been well paid for his work, or asking why he drank so much.

He did not, in fact, drink a great deal; but with his quivering, electric temperament he could get, with four glasses, into a state which more stolid men would not reach with five bottles. Once, and only once, when too much of this public insult had made him reckless, he answered back. He was playing Othello across the water at his usual fee of fifty pounds a night. The audience did not hoot or hiss him, or throw things. It more or less ignored him, and gave its applause to the Iago. But at the end of the play it called for him. He came forward, and told it that he had played at all the principal theatres of England and America, and had never appeared before "such a set of ignorant brutes" as those he then saw.

Actors and actresses had not only to work well for their masters but to work hard. Theatres opened at six, and went on till midnight. The bill was usually a triple bill: a one-act play, a Shakespeare or other drama, and then a farce. At nine o'clock the public was admitted at half-price. The cast usually had to appear in two of the pieces, and "utility men" had to appear in all three. Kean, long after his early triumphs in London, would do Richard or Othello or Lear, and then appear in the farce as Harlequin, or would do songs and imitations in the after-piece. The theatre at that time was very much a living thing in the life of the people, and they kept the actors up to the mark.

But it is curious that at a time when it was so much alive with strong and vivid actors, it was so empty of authors. Rich in histrionics, it was sterile in plays. It added nothing to the repertory of English drama. It gave the stage the Kembles and their sister, Sarah Siddons; G. F. Cooke; Munden; Elliston; Bannister; Edmund Kean; Macready; but not a play whose title conveys anything to us. It was like that through almost the whole century. Between *The School for Scandal* and *The Importance of Being Earnest* one finds nothing that is performed to-day. Which seems to show what I have often suspected—that the actor's art flourishes on poor plays.

Exciting nights at the theatre, in the very early years of the century, were provided by two actors who flitted briefly across the stage and disappeared; one, a young prodigy, the other a pitiful freak.

The response of theatre-goers to the appearances of Master William Betty, the Infant Roscius, shows that the mind of the theatre-goer was much as it is to-day. In town and country they fought and struggled to see that not very accomplished boy as they do to-day when some inane film-performer attends a first-night. He appeared first in Belfast; then in Dublin; then in Glasgow and Edinburgh. His first appearance in England was at Birmingham, and there the madness began.

A few days before his first performance, all hotels and inns were filled. When it was known that he had arrived, his hotel was besieged, and he was pursued about the streets. Similar scenes attended his arrival in Sheffield, Liverpool, and other towns where he was booked.

When his engagement for London was announced (his terms at Covent Garden were fifty guineas a night and a benefit; at Drury Lane they were fifty pounds a night for three nights, and a hundred pounds for every other night), theatre-goers went so crazy that some of them stayed in the theatre the night before, hiding under the seats. Crowds began to gather at the doors in the morning, and by mid-day there was such a mass all round the theatre, that not only were groups of constables stationed at different points, but a company of Guards was brought out to keep order.

At each appearance this nonsense was repeated and sometimes intensified. One afternoon, when the crowd was tired of waiting at the doors, it broke them down, smashed windows, and poured in with so much violence that staircases were broken and the box office barrier torn down. He became the darling of Society, a new toy for the witless. He was taken here and there about the Court and to all the great houses. When he rode out crowds pressed about him to touch him. A sitting of the Commons was actually adjourned so that members might attend one of his performances. For twenty-eight London appearances, in which he played Romeo, Young Norval, Hamlet, and characters in forgotten plays, he received over £4,000.

All that tumult caused, and in twelve months a fortune of £30,000 realised, by a pretty boy of fourteen, whose talent was as slender as his figure. His career was short. At seventeen he retired with his fortune, and his father sent him to Cambridge. But at twenty-two he came out again. He was then awkward and over-grown, and his voice was not good. But still, for a time, he managed to get packed houses, and to increase his fortune. Then his appeal ceased, and he went into complete retirement, and lived so long that when he died nobody was alive who knew that he had been an actor. He died at eighty-three.

The other sensation was only a matter of months. It centred on the appearances of an inept and eccentric amateur, Robert Coates, in his own productions of *Romeo and Juliet*, in which he played Romeo. Coates had been born in Antigua. He came to England in middle life, with some means, and settled at Bath, where he played the beau. He was then about thirty-six, but looked much older. His face is described as sallow and much wrinkled, and his general expression was a cunning grin. His dress was notable for its display. In the morning he went about in richly-furred coats, whatever the weather; in the evening he wore a coat and waistcoat with diamond buttons, and diamond buckles on his shoes. After a time it was announced that he, a Distinguished Amateur, would appear at the theatre in the part of Romeo.

Those who had seen him and talked with him had recognised a complete fool. Naturally, all Bath turned out that night and packed the theatre, expecting to witness a failure. The actual performance was much more than that. The first laughter was caused by his costume. He wore a cloak of sky-blue silk, covered with spangles; red pantaloons; a vest of white muslin with a huge cravat; a Stuart wig; and an opera hat. The costume in all parts was too tight, and the few gestures he knew could be made only with much trouble. So tight was it that, unknown to himself, the back seam of the pantaloons was rent and showed a good wisp of shirt, so that every turn he made brought a roar of laughter. His awkward movements, his sheepish way of standing, his general expression—which was a grin and a nod—and his harsh voice, together brought unceasing laughter from the audience. None of this at all disturbed him. Captain Gronow was present, and left an account of the sorry affair:

> The balcony scene was interrupted by shrieks of laughter, for in the midst of one of Juliet's impassioned exclamations, Romeo quietly took out his snuff-box and applied a pinch to his nose; on this a wag in the gallery bawled out, "I say, Romeo, give us a pinch," when the impassioned lover, in the most affected manner, walked to the side boxes and offered the contents of his box first to the gentlemen, and then with great gallantry to the ladies. . . . Romeo then returned to the balcony, and was seen to extend his arms; but all passed in dumb show, so incessant were the shouts of laughter. . . .
>
> The amateur actor showed many indications of aberration of mind, and seemed rather the object of pity than of amusement; he, however, appeared delighted with himself, and also with his audience. . . .
>
> The dying scene was irresistibly comic, and I question if Liston, Munden, or Joey Knight was ever greeted with such merriment; for Romeo dragged the unfortunate Juliet from the tomb, much in the same manner as a washer-woman thrusts into her cart the bag of foul linen. But how shall I describe his death? Out came a dirty silk handkerchief from his pocket, with which he carefully swept the ground; then his opera hat was carefully placed for a pillow, and down he laid himself. After various tossings about, he seemed reconciled to the position; but the house vociferously bawled "Die again, Romeo!" and, obedient to the command, he rose up and went through the ceremony again.

A third death was then demanded, and he was about to comply when the unfortunate actress who was his Juliet—a professional—having had enough of it, got up from the tomb and brought the curtain down with an adapted line from the play:

> Dying is such sweet sorrow,
> That he would die again until to-morrow.

He was satisfied that he had made such an impression as entitled him to a London hearing, and a little later he took the Haymarket Theatre, and repeated his performance. But London found him more tedious than amusing, and even as a curiosity a few appearances exhausted his interest. Thereafter he contented himself with making a figure in the park by driving about in a barouche designed like a cockle-shell and drawn by two milk-white steeds; and with plunging heavily at gaming-tables.

The gaming-table continued to be as great an attraction to our old and young nobility as in the early days of White's. Its rival for their interest was the ring, and young sprigs of the peerage felt honoured at being admitted to the intimacy of bruisers such as Cribb, Belcher, Tom Spring, and Jackson, and delighted in spending their evenings with them. Tom Cribb kept the Union Arms, in Panton Street, corner of Oxendon Street; and Belcher for a time kept the Castle, in Holborn, where he was succeeded as landlord by Tom Spring. At each of them was a special room for favoured customers decorated with sporting prints and with the cups and other trophies won by the champions. At Belcher's was kept the Daffy Club (a slang term for gin), a gathering of the Fancy and their backers and the sporting reporters. It is described by Charles Westmacott:

> To see the place in perfection, a stranger should choose the night previous to some important mill, when our host of the Castle plays second, and all the lads are mustered to stump up their blunt, or to catch the important whisper where the scene of action is likely to be. . . .
> The long room is neatly fitted up, and lighted with *gas*; and the numerous sporting subjects elegantly framed and glazed, have rather an imposing effect upon the entrance of the visitor. . . . The long table, or the ring, as it is facetiously termed, is where the old standers generally perch themselves to receive the visits of the swells, and give each other the office relative to passing events; and what set of men are better able to speak of society in all its various ramifications, from the cabinet-counsellor to the costermonger? . . . Our host, a civil, well-behaved man, without any of the exterior appearance of the ruffian, or perhaps I should say of his profession, and with all the good-natured qualifications for a peaceable citizen and an obliging, merry landlord; next to him you will perceive the immortal typo, the all-accomplished Pierce Egan . . . Tom Spring, who is fond of cocking as well as fighting, is seen with his bag in the right-hand corner.

Another description is given in Moore's *Tom Cribb's Memorial*:

> Last Friday night a bang-up set
> Of milling blades at Belcher's met,
> All high-bred heroes of the Ring,
> Whose very gammon would delight one,
> Who, nursed beneath the Fancy's wing,
> Show all her feathers but the white one.

> Brave Tom, the champion, with an air
> Almost Corinthian, took the chair,
> And kept the coves in quiet tune
> By showing such a fist of mutton
> As on a point of order soon
> Would take the shine from Speaker Sutton.

In the 1820's gaming among the wealthy was given a great impetus—which it hardly needed—by the establishment of Crockford's. Numbers of poor modern representatives of "great families" owe their condition, first, to the idiocy of their ancestors of over a century ago, and second, to Crockford, who provided the means for the exhibition of the idiocy on a larger scale than any other "banker." However large the transactions in the betting-books and at the tables of White's and Brooks' and Watier's had been, they were all eclipsed by the play at Crockford's. Whole estates were lost there in one night, and during the thirties many a broken aristocrat was sauntering about Calais and Boulogne and the German spas who, a short time before, had been drawing a grand income from the family property. Gronow says of Crockford that he:

> ... won the whole of the ready money of the then existing generation. As is often the case at Lord's Cricket ground, the great match of the gentlemen of England against the professional players was won by the latter. It was a very hollow thing, and in a few years twelve hundred thousand pounds were swept away by the fortunate fishmonger.

Crockford began life as a fishmonger, and kept a shop in the Strand. He was then a betting man in a small way, and after one or two lucky strokes he took a share in a bank which operated at Watier's Club. This went well until one night, when it went even better. He and his partner, in a twenty-four hour session, cleared one hundred thousand pounds. Upon that, he resigned his partnership, and built his own club-house at the top of St. James' Street, where the Devonshire now stands, furnished it with all magnificence, and engaged as chef the famous Ude, chef to the Duke of York. This was Crockford's, sometimes called Crocky's, but more generally Fishmonger's Hall, in allusion to his origin. One of his rules was that nobody could be a member unless he was already a member of White's, Brooks', Boodle's, the Cocoa Tree, the Alfred, or the Travellers', though if a young man of great fortune was introduced the rule was lifted.

Most of the peerage belonged to Crockford's; all foreign ambassadors were made members, and all distinguished visitors from Europe. The Duke of Wellington was a member; and Talleyrand and Esterhazy; and Disraeli and Bulwer Lytton and D'Orsay. The superb suppers, with

42 The Royal Saloon, Piccadilly

43 "The Cyprians' Ball at the Argyle Rooms"

44 "The Daffy Club, or Musical Muster of the Fancy"

Plates by Robert Cruikshank, from "The English Spy" (1826)

45 "Play at Crockford's. Count D'Orsay calling a Main"
From a contemporary illustration

46 Ladies Gambling
From a drawing of ca. 1810

noble wines, were served without charge, and the supper-table was cleared and re-set half a dozen times between midnight and morning. At that table, Gronow says:

"Crockford's." By George Cruikshank

... the most brilliant sallies of wit, the most agreeable conversation, the most interesting anecdotes, interspersed with grave political discussions and acute logical reasoning on every conceivable subject, proceeded from the soldiers, scholars, statesmen, poets, and men of pleasure, who, when the house was up, and balls and parties at an end, delighted to finish their evening with a little supper and a good deal of hazard at old Crocky's ... there Horace Twiss made proof of an appetite, and Edward Montague of a thirst which astonished all beholders; whilst the bitter jests of Sir Joseph Copley, Col. Armstrong, and John Wilson Croker, and the brilliant wit of Alvanley were the delight of all present. . . . But the brightest medal has its reverse, and after all the wit and gaiety and excitement of the night, how disagreeable the waking up, and how very unpleasant the sight of the little card, with its numerous figures marked down on the debtor side. . . .

All around St. James Street and Jermyn Street and Pall Mall were smaller and illegal gaming-rooms, where anybody would be admitted and stakes were low. These were called Silver Hells. Gaming at clubs such as White's and Crockford's was a private affair and not subject to the law; but these places were not clubs, and so were liable to be raided. Many of them had four or five doors. The front door had a wicket through which the caller was scrutinised. If he knew the word he was admitted, and found himself face to face with a iron grille. If he could satisfy the watch-dog the grille was unlocked and he passed into a passage where was a green baize door, also locked. Before he reached the tables he had to pass a number of these doors, so that Bow Street men had little chance of surprising a party in the act of illegal play. If a Bow Street man did get in, and the watch-dog was not satisfied with him, he merely stepped on a particular spot of a mat which covered a spring and gave an alarm in the play-room. By the time he and the visitor reached the play-room, all they saw was a number of men sitting round the fire enjoying their bottles. Not a sign of card, counter, dice, baize table, or money was to be seen.

Song-and-supper rooms, on the lines of the Coal Hole and the Cyder Cellar (Thackeray's "Cave of Harmony") began to appear in all parts, and they all had fancy names. Surtees makes John Jorrocks a prominent figure in many of them—Chairman of the Incorporated Society of Good Fellows; Recorder of the Wide-Awake Club; and President of the Sublime Free-and-Easy. It was from these spontaneous entertainments that the most popular entertainment of the later years of the century developed. As they became more and more crowded, the owners of the public-houses in which they were held built annexes which were used solely for the concerts. These were the first Music Halls, and they then gave only song and music. A little later, fully-equipped theatres were built for a somewhat similar, but more elaborate and more varied entertainment: the Theatres of Variety. When, in the twentieth century, these began to lose their appeal, a new thing was offered. At least, the public thought it was Continental and new, but actually it was very English and old. As the appeal of the music-halls declined, the hotels and restaurants offered supper-cabaret; thus making a full circle in midnight entertainment from the 1920's back to the 1820's.

In the *Sketches by Boz* Dickens gives a description of a song-and-supper room or Harmonic Meeting. The favourite supper dishes were oysters, kidneys, chops, and Welsh rabbits. He describes the room as a lofty room with a top table and two long supporting tables. About eighty or a hundred guests (all men) are seated at the tables, applauding the singers by banging with their pewter mugs or the handles of their knives:

> They are applauding a glee, which has just been executed by the three "professional gentlemen" at the top of the centre table, one of whom is in the chair—the little pompous man with the bald head just emerging from the collar of his green coat. The others are seated on either side of him—the stout man with the small voice, and the thin-faced dark man in black. The little man in the chair is a most amusing personage—such condescending grandeur, and such a voice! . . .
> "Pray give your orders, gen'l'm'n—pray give your orders," says the pale-faced man with the red head; and demands for "goes" of gin and "goes" of

brandy, and pints of stout, and cigars of peculiar mildness, are vociferously made from all parts of the room. . . . "Gen'l'men," says the little pompous man, accompanying the word with a knock of the president's hammer on the table—"Gen'l'men, allow me to claim your attention—our friend, Mr. Smuggins, will oblige." "Bravo!" shout the company; and Smuggins, after a considerable quantity of coughing by way of symphony, and a most facetious sniff or two, which afford general delight, sings a comic song, with a fal-de-ral, tol-de-rol chorus at the end of every verse, much longer than the verse itself.

A Public-house Sing-song in the early Nineteenth Century

Taverns in every district held their harmonic meetings, some nightly, some once a week. There were numbers of them in the eastern suburbs—Whitechapel, Wapping, Ratcliff and Shoreditch—and across the river in Southwark and Lambeth. Shoreditch, indeed, appropriately, as the home of London's first theatre, had a cheap and crude night-life, of its own in the way of harmonic meetings, penny gaffs, galanty shows, and slap-bang supper-rooms.

One of the best-known song-and-supper houses at the western end was Offley's, in Covent Garden. Its dining-room was the largest of its kind, and it prided itself on its chops and its strong Burton ale. It had no decorations or elaborate furniture. The walls were bare; the table appointments were serviceable earthenware or pewter. Everything about the place took its note from the food and the cooking—plain and good. If the singing, led off by Offley himself, wasn't good, it was by all accounts hearty; so hearty that, as the place backed on to St. Paul's churchyard, the supper-room was fitted with double windows. Another famous place, which remained famous up to the 1870's, was the mansion near by, in King Street, which in 1774, was London's first family hotel, and in our own time housed the National Sporting Club. In the 1820's it was taken over from its then proprietor, a man named Joy, by Evans, formerly of the Cyder Cellar. He turned it into a supper and singing room; not, as elsewhere, for sing-songs, but for supper accompanied by solos and glees from genuine professionals. Near it was another place, the Finish, which Charles Westmacott describes:

> How many jovial nights have I passed and jolly fellows have I met in the snug sanctum sanctorum, a little crib, as the flashmongers would call it, with an entrance through the bar, and into which none were ever permitted to enter without a formal introduction and the gracious permission of the hostess.... Here poor Tom Sheridan, with a comic gravity that set discretion at defiance, would let fly some of his brilliant drolleries at the improvisatore, Theodore Hook; who, lacking nothing of his opponent's wit, would quickly return his fire with the sharp encounter of a satiric epigram or a brace of puns.... Here, too, I remember to have seen for the first time in my life the wayward Byron, with the light of genius beaming in his noble countenance, and an eye brilliant and expressive as the evening star; the rich juice of the Tuscan grape had diffused an unusual glow over his features, and inspired him with a playful animation. An histrionic star alike distinguished for talent and eccentricity accompanied him—the gallant, gay Lothario, Kean.

Night-life at any time has much the same general features, but one feature of that time is missing from ours. In certain districts—Covent Gárden, Drury Lane, Haymarket, Long Acre—the wanderer at midnight might encounter at a street corner a watchman carrying a pole with a board attached to it, bearing the legend—Beware Bad Houses. These men were sent out by the churchwardens of the parish, and their purpose was not only to warn, but to stop men from entering that particular street, and thus, by lack of custom, to drive the inhabitants out. They were seldom successful; their boards often had the effect of a free advertisement upon the young and giddy of that time, whose spirit then, and through most of the nineteenth century, was expressed in one of the tavern choruses:

> We're jovial, happy, and gay, boys!
> We rise with the moon, which is surely full soon,
> Sing with the owl, our tutelar fowl,
> Laugh and joke at your go-to-bed folk,
> Never think but what we shall drink,
> Never care but on what we shall fare—
> Turning the night into day, boys!

47 "Sporting a Toe among the Corinthians at Almacks in the West"

48 The Saloon at Covent Garden

49 A Masquerade Supper at the Opera House

Plates by Isaac and George Cruikshank, from "Life in London" (1821)

50 "Beware of Bad Houses!"

A considerable literature of London night-life began to appear. With brighter streets, the practice mentioned in the last line of the song was spreading among all classes, and those who made it their business to cater for it saw that the more it spread, the more money for them. They therefore encouraged it by song, story, and all those means which we to-day lump under one ugly word—propaganda. There were Guides to night-resorts; Exposures of night-resorts and the London sinks; Rambles round the night-resorts; all cheap imitations of those successful and rather expensive works, Pierce Egan's *Life in London*, Westmacott's *English Spy*, *Real Life in London*, and so on.

Most of them were shabby, humbugging things, pretending to condemn what they were advertising. One or two even achieved the apparently impossible distinction of being written in a worse English than Pierce Egan's. But they helped to bring custom to the night-resorts, and to continue the effect of Pierce Egan's book and the dramatisation of it, in drawing young squirelings to the town. His and Westmacott's books are read to-day only by students seeking sidelights on the life of a small and rackety section. They do not present *real* life in London; only that small section; and while the facts at hand were rich enough, one suspects that even those they often exaggerated. First editions of the books command high prices to-day, not on account of the authors but on account of the spirited coloured plates of the Cruikshanks. Those of *The English Spy* are wholly by Robert; and the majority of those of *Life in London* are also his. George did only a few. J. C. Hotten says that Robert amused himself by putting actual portraits into the plates. In all the plates to *The English Spy*, the figure of Bob Transit is a portrait of himself, and the figure of Bernard Blackmantle is Westmacott. In the plates to *Life in London*, the figure of Corinthian Tom is a portrait of George; Jerry Hawthorn is Robert himself, and Bob Logic is a portrait of Pierce Egan. All three were living then much the night-life they described and sketched, and were mixing it with hard work. Robert and Egan went on living it, and it seems to have done them little harm. Robert reached the age of sixty-seven and Egan seventy-seven. George dropped the life quite early, and became teetotal and respectable, and lasted nearly twenty years longer than his brother as a pernickety person and an intemperate temperance advocate.

We get glimpses of night-life of all kinds in country and in town in that contemporary encyclopaedia of manners and customs—*Pickwick*. There are the ball-nights at "Ba-a-ath," under Cyrus Angelo Bantam; "moments snatched from Paradise; rendered bewitching by music, beauty, elegance, fashion, etiquette, and—and—above all, by the absence of tradespeople, who are quite inconsistent with Paradise." There was the dinner and garrison ball at Rochester. There were the nights at Eatanswill, each with its incidental adventure. There was Sam Weller's "sworry" at Bath, and there was the party given by Benjamin Allen and Bob Sawyer in Lant Street, which broke up in disorder at two in the morning. And there were the Christmas carousals at Dingley Dell, with their bowls of punch, their songs and tales and dances and difficult journeys to bed.

Despite the festivity that accompanied those nights, they were light and mild by comparison with the earlier nights described in the clumsy sketches of Pierce Egan. But in one of the Boz sketches, *Making a Night of It*, Dickens is in the Egan vein. Two young clerks, drawing their quarter's salary, agree to celebrate. They begin with a little dinner—four chops and four kidneys, stout, and bread and cheese and walnuts. Then come Scotch whisky and Havanas, one "go" followed by another, until one of them begins to feel "very much as if he had been sitting in a hackney-coach with his back to the horses," and goes to sleep. After his recovery, they go at half-price to the City Theatre, where the quiet one again goes to sleep, while his friend, affected in the opposite way, addresses the gallery, interrupts the actors, imitates the singers, and makes all the farmyard noises he can reproduce. They are finally thrown out by the ushers, and adjourn to a wine-vaults, and drink brandy and soda, and treat everybody in the place, and after further adventures of knocking down five men, four boys and three women, and wrenching off five door-knockers and two bell-handles, and giving several alarms of fire, and assaulting the police, they finish the night in the cells, and in the morning have to pay thirty-four pounds.

During the twenties and thirties the club became a more prominent feature of social life and more widespread. It was about this time that some of the great clubs existing to-day were formed and their premises built in Pall Mall and Piccadilly. They developed club-life as we ourselves know it. They were not mere dining-clubs or clubs for gaming. They were the home from home, where men of like position and interests could meet for general intercourse, and live more cheaply than at restaurants or even in their own houses. The Union was built in 1824; the University in 1826; the Oriental in 1827; then followed the Oxford and Cambridge, 1828, the Windham, 1828, Athenaeum, 1830, Garrick, 1831, Carlton, 1836, and Reform, 1838.

In some respects the life was a little different from that of to-day. It was more free and intimate. Dining at your club to-day is much the same as dining at a public restaurant; half the members are strangers to you. But at that time the club was not an assembly of units. It was a close group, all the members of which knew each other. In the evenings talk was general, and midnights were convivial. Nights at the Athenaeum must have been of a kind that would surprise and no doubt bore the members of to-day. One has only to recall that a prominent member of that now-august institution was Theodore Hook. . . . A sharp contrast to the wicked stories told about it in our own time. The story, for example, of the member who approached another and said: "Pardon me, have you done with *The Times*?" Whereupon the member addressed burst into tears. The first man, in some concern, asked the cause of his distress, and got the answer: "Forgive my weakness, but I've been a member of this club for twenty-two years, and this is the first time anybody's said a word to me." And another—the member ringing for a waiter, and asking: "Will you get that gentleman in the corner chair taken away? To my certain knowledge he's been dead two days." The waiter ordered the porter to get it done, but the wrong member was removed and laid out; and it wasn't till the waiter went back to the room an hour later that the mistake was noticed.

In Hook's day he had a particular table in the corner of the dining-room, and around it gathered a nightly audience of bishops and others, anxious to catch some of his talk. The corner was known as Temperance Corner. Hook's habits being what they were, and bishops being what they were, he did not like, in their presence, to keep calling for brandy and water. So his order, repeated many times through the evening, was for a jug of "toast-and-water."

There is a description of one of his club days and nights which displays his abounding physical energy. He would rise late, and dash at his literary work. Towards dinner-time he would drive to one of his clubs, and there sit talking on brandy-and-water. Then he would drive to another, and do the same thing. Then on to a third where he had a committee meeting. He would take the chair, address the members, show the accounts, pass them, propose a vote of thanks to himself, second it and carry it. Then off to another club to dine. To another to supper; and then a long sitting in Temperance Corner with the "toast-and-water." Another story concerns his being at the Garrick Club in the summer and expressing a wish for a long, cold drink. A member recommended the club's very own gin-punch, made from a secret recipe. A jug was made for him, and he pronounced it good, and asked for a second. The second was followed by a third; then a fourth, with a chop or two; then a fifth, and eventually a sixth. After which he went off to keep a dinner engagement.

None of his recorded witticisms are very good; they have not the sting of those of Rogers or the playfulness of Lamb's. Unless the best things were lost on the air, Temperance Corner heard nothing like Lamb's little things such as his remark at a tavern-supper to a young poet who had been holding forth on the beauty of his own verses: "What I like about you is that you've no m-mock modesty. Nor r-real either." Or his remark at dinner to a woman who had been boring him with a eulogy of some noble lord, his brilliant talk, his charm, his exquisite manners; ending with: "You see, I know him, bless him." "Do you?" said Lamb; "well, I don't, so damn him just for luck." The typical Hook witticism is illustrated by his justification of his habits. A friend met him at Crockford's at three in the morning. He was drinking brandy. "But I thought," the friend said, "that you'd been very ill." "So I have." "Then you oughtn't to be here." "Oh, yes. I'm obeying doctor's orders. He told me to be very careful not to expose myself to the night air. So I come up here to dinner, and make it a rule on no account to go home before five in the morning."

As clubs began to multiply in London and country, they had their critics and their defenders. The critics considered that they were likely to break up the family evening and destroy home life. Thomas Hood turned this criticism into facetious verse:

> Alas for those departed days
> Of social wedded life,
> When married folks had married ways,
> And lived like man and wife.
> Oh, wedlock then was picked by none,
> As safe a lock as Chubb's.
> But couples that should be as one
> Are now the Two of Clubs.

Thomas Walker, of the *Original*, in which, among many other topics, he set down the principles of aristology, or the art of dining, entered for the defence. Clubs, he held, offered an economical way of living, on the co-operative principle; they gave the man of small means the mansion of a lord and the servants of such a mansion; they gave him the library of a great mansion and the kitchen of a great mansion. As for their drawing men to neglect their families, he found by observation at one particular club that in the evening hours usually given to "female" society, there were not twenty members in the rooms. Clubs, he insisted, so far from spoiling a man for home life, gave him a training

51 The Progress of Victorian Intemperance: the Relapse

52 "From the Gin-shop to the Dancing-rooms, the poor girl is driven on in that course which ends in misery"
From "The Drunkard's Children," by George Cruikshank

53 "Lift me up!—Tie me in my chair!—Fill my glass"
An illustration from "Jorrocks's Jaunts and Jollities"

54 "Mr. Jorrocks's Lecture on 'Unting"

for it. It showed him the virtue of economy, temperance, forbearance, and order.

Mrs. Gore, the fashionable novelist of her day, was more acid, and perhaps nearer to reality, in her approval of clubs. She saw them as useful lightning-conductors of domestic storms:

> The man forced to remain at home and vent his crossness on his wife and children is a much worse animal to bear with than the man who grumbles his way to Pall Mall, and, not daring to swear at the club servants, or knock about the club furniture, becomes socialised into decency. Nothing like the subordination exercised in a community of equals for reducing a fiery temper.

A somewhat similar point was made in our own time by the American writer, Don Marquis, in the days of American prohibition of liquor. His character, The Old Soak, defending the saloon, illustrated its value in cases of domestic quarrel. Under prohibition, the husband, after an overnight or morning upheaval with his wife, would go off to the office and brood upon it at intervals all through the day, and return in the evening with the same grouch on him. Whereas, in the days before prohibition, he would go off in the morning burning with resentment, and on the way to the office would drop into his favourite saloon, take a drink, and discuss his domestic problem with the always-sympathetic bar-tender. They would compare notes on the subject of women, and the bar-tender would have one with him, and then offer him one on the house. By the time he reached the office the cloud of that domestic row had been dissipated, and he would go home in the evening full of love and kindness, and with no hang-over of the morning's duel.

Evenings at the watering and seaside places still offered little more than they had done for years past. There were assembly rooms, raffles, and lotteries, and visitors to the rooms would sometimes oblige the company with a song. Surtees' description of a night at Margate, in *Jorrocks's Jaunts* (1838), is no doubt typical of nights at similar places. Jorrocks and his friends Jemmy Green and the Yorkshireman strolled out to see the sights soon after sunset:

> One turn to the shore, and the gas-lights of the town drew back the party like moths to the streets, which were literally swarming with the population. Cheapside at three o'clock in the afternoon, as Mr. Jorrocks observed, was never fuller than Margate streets that evening. All was lighted up—all brilliant and all gay—care seemed banished from every countenance, and pretty faces and smart gowns reigned in its stead. . . . Having perambulated the streets, the sound of music attracted Jemmy Green's attention, and our party turned into a long, crowded, and brilliantly-lighted bazaar, just as the last notes of a barrel organ at the far end faded away, and a young woman in a hat and feathers, with a swan's-down muff and tippet, was handed by a

very smart young man in dirty-white Berlin gloves, and an equally soiled white waistcoat, into a sort of orchestra above, where, after the plaudits of the company had subsided, she struck up.

Between the songs there were raffles, at a shilling a ticket, for a "genteel rosewood perfume-box," a set of crimping-irons, a workbox with a view of Margate on the lid, six sherry labels, a snuff-box, a coral rattle, a silk yard-measure and a dozen bodkins with silver eyes. The sale of ten tickets was necessary before the raffle could begin, and each holder of a ticket made three throws with the dice, the highest total score being the winner. Songs were given for the entertainment of the company by those who could sing, and some who couldn't, in return for raffle tickets. One or two similar bazaars and a dancing hall provided the rest of the evening amusement for the town's visitors. After an hour or so of raffle and song, Jorrocks and his friends at eleven o'clock sat down to the hotel supper—shrimps, lobsters, broiled bones, fried ham, and poached eggs; followed by a quart and a half of old port, mulled with lemon, cloves, sugar, and cinnamon.

Dickens, in one of the Boz sketches, presents a similar scene of night-life at Ramsgate. The chief rendezvous seems to have been the Library, where the entertainment followed the usual course of raffles, lotteries, and concert. Indeed, the two scenes might have been taken one from the other:

> The Library was crowded. . . . There were young ladies in maroon-coloured gowns and black velvet bracelets, dispensing fancy articles in the shop, and presiding over games of chance in the concert-room. There were marriageable daughters, and marriage-making mammas, gaming and promenading, and turning over music, and flirting. There were some male beaux doing the sentimental in whispers, and others doing the ferocious in moustache. . . . "Who's this?" inquired Mr. Cymon Tuggs, of Mrs. Captain Waters, as a short female, in a blue velvet hat and feathers, was led into the orchestra by a fat man in black tights and cloudy Berlins. "Mrs. Tippin, of the London theatres," replied Belinda, referring to the programme of the concert.

Night-life in the sporting countries was, as Harriette Wilson complained, generally sluggish. It was a matter of dining, and of long sitting over the port, while each man recounted at tedious length some "tremendous run" of the past. After reading reports of some of those evenings one feels that one could almost endure one of those insane and often disgusting nights at Halston, in Shropshire, where Jack Mytton was squire.

Mytton spent his days and nights in committing suicide, but it took him thirty-eight years to accomplish it. In every way open to a man

55 John Mytton shows: "How to cross a Country comfortably after Dinner".
From the plate by Alken and Rawlins in "Memoirs of the Life of John Mytton".

he risked his neck, his limbs, and his health. In the hunting-field he took lunatic jumps. In the hardest winter he wore the same clothes as in summer—no underclothes, a light jacket, and white linen trousers without lining. He went wildfowl shooting, in the frozen dusk, in nothing but his shirt, and once, because his clothes impeded him when engaged in that sport, he took them off and crawled naked across the ice to a point which offered cover. In trying out a new horse, he harnessed it to his gig, and, to see if the horse was a jumper, he sent horse and gig at a five-barred gate and cleared it without smashing the gig. He could not swim, but he would constantly plunge on horseback into the deepest river and somehow get across. A bad fall in the hunting-field broke three ribs. Next morning, when he was in bed, a friend called and hoped it would be a lesson to him. He at once got up, got out his horse and joined in a hunt. Under the intense pain he fainted three times, but he finished the run. Every day he drank six bottles of port, until he tired of it and changed to brandy. He died in the King's Bench prison, penniless and demented.

That Shropshire lad made the Shropshire nights of his time as noisy as those of any London night-cellar of to-day. They are recorded by C. J. Apperley (Nimrod) in his *Life of John Mytton*, and they are what one would expect of such a character. He was not without education; he was well read in the classics, and often came out with an apposite quotation. But he was, like many educated men of that Corinthian time, a man born out of his class. He had the tastes of the lout. Sometimes his moods carried him beyond the lout. Two or three of Apperley's anecdotes of his behaviour show him as a wild beast who should not have been at large, and was only at large because of his wealth. He came of a long line of landed gentry, but, like any parvenu, considered that any insult or assault on poor people could be wiped out with a few guineas.

One of his notions of entertaining his evening company was to ride into the dining-room on a bear which nobody but himself could control, and then stop controlling it. His notion of a lark was to make a guest drunk, and have him put to bed in a locked room with the bear and two bull-dogs. One night, when two respectable men had been his guests, he saw them off at the door, then went to the stables, put on a smock and mask, mounted a fast horse, cut across country, and met them at a cross-road with "Stand and Deliver!" and fired on them. Next day he entertained his evening company with an account of their fright, and the speed their horses made in getting away from him.

One of his midnight exploits was a ride across country in a gig drawn by two horses harnessed tandem. He told the company where he had been dining that he knew of a short way home, and made a bet that he would take it. To do it he had to get horses and gig over two fields, a sunk fence three yards wide, a broad drain, and two fences with ditches on either side. A number of servants were sent out to the fields, with lanterns to light the awkward points, and Mytton made a start. The gig got stuck in the sunk fence, but he lashed the horses out of it. Horses and gig cleared the drain, flinging Mytton from the driver's seat on to the back of the rear horse; but he climbed back to his seat, got the reins, and jumped horses and gig over the other two fences. Another night, by way of amusing a supper party, he loosed two or three young foxes in the dining-room. A little later, between circuits of the bottle, he introduced a Spanish bull-dog and an English mastiff, and set them at each other. When the mastiff was getting the worse, he grabbed the bull-dog (its weight was seventy pounds), fixed his teeth in the scruff of its neck, and held it suspended in mid-air.

One turns with relief from savages of this sort to the good company that assembled at night, in the 'twenties and 'thirties, at two famous London houses. The centre of politics (Whig), literature, and wit was Holland House. An invitation to that house was as much prized by one kind of man as a ticket for Almack's by an inferior kind. It was a recognition of your arrival, not as a social figure but as a man of gifts and qualities. From 1836 to 1849 the Blessington and D'Orsay menage at Gore House attracted somewhat similar company, and gave lavish entertainment; but they never seriously challenged the other house. Lady Blessington was a social figure, but she was not in the sacred circle of society. It was commonly said that she got only Lady Holland's siftings; men went to Gore House who could not get invitations from the other. Still, she had Louis Napoleon, whose cause D'Orsay nursed along when it was without much hope, and, in his time of need, received the usual reward. And she had Campbell, and James and Horace Smith, and Theodore Hook; Bulwer Lytton, Washington Irving, the young Disraeli, the young Thackeray, the young Dickens, and Landor.

Perhaps because she and D'Orsay were flouting convention by living in the same house (he was married to, and parted from, her stepdaughter) her nights were touched with an air of Latin freedom not found in the regal Holland House. It is quite likely that the literary men and wits found her nights, paste as they might have been, more agreeable than the first-water nights at the greater house. Blessington was herself a novelist (of a sort) and editor of *Keepsakes* and other annuals, and they probably got on better with her than with the stately and domineering hostess of Holland House. ("Macaulay, we've had enough of that subject. Talk about something else.") At the Holland table appeared Lord Brougham, Lord Thurlow, Lord Lyndhurst, Lord Jeffrey, Lord Aberdeen, the duc d'Orleans, Talleyrand, Metternich, Mme de Stael, Lord John Russell, Sydney Smith, Macaulay, Grattan, the Duke of Clarence, Thomas Moore. Yes; nights to be remembered and set down in diaries. But for nights to be enjoyed, most of us, I think, would choose the other house, if Sydney Smith and Talleyrand could be borrowed from across the road.

Moore's *Journal* is dotted with references to his nights at Holland House; but then, as Byron said, "Tommy dearly loves a lord," and he would naturally have preferred a company of ribbons and garters and stars to a company of his colleagues. He was fastidious in this and in another matter. On receiving an invitation to a house he had not visited, he would do what most of us would like to do if we dared, and so save ourselves from many a tedious occasion. He would go round to people who knew the prospective host, and would want to know what sort of kitchen the man kept; whether he had a good chef and a good cellar; what kind of dishes he usually served and how they were prepared; and whether he got his wines direct from Bordeaux and Burgundy or through a dealer. And he would want to know what sort of company the man kept, and would even go so far as to make known his wishes (like Royalty) as to what other guests should be invited to meet him. When all these points had been answered to his satisfaction, he would accept; if they were not, he would decline; and his company was so much desired that many houses were ready to fall in with his whims. I doubt, however, that Lady Holland would have stood any of that nonsense from him.

Nights of the Holland House and Gore House kind are seldom known to-day. We have hot parties, and snappy talk, and a succession of arrivals and departures, but it would be difficult now to gather a company from all distinguished ways of life, to be at their best and talk on their particular subject, and to keep together for seven or eight hours. That kind of night passed with the coming of the railway. When people could move quickly from town to country, and from city to city, hostesses found themselves faced with many blank nights. The company they had once collected was scattering itself all over England. Speed killed many things besides human bodies. It killed leisure, and with it conversation, to which leisure is essential. In our own time, with so many new devices for speed, we are suffering in acute form the disease which in the early railway age was only chronic. Our friends now not only refuse to sit and talk for four or five hours, or even one hour; they are so busy going everywhere that they have no time to be anywhere.

In the second half of the century the theatre became more and more the chief evening amusement; and for the less fastidious there was the music-hall. Hood's little piece of trick-rhyming on the London evening, though written of an earlier period, suggests the natural turn of thoughts at that hour:

> Even is come, and from the dark Park, hark!
> The signal of the setting sun—one gun;
> And six is sounding from the chime; prime time
> To go and see the Drury Lane Dane slain—
> Or hear Othello's jealous doubt spout out—
> Or Macbeth raving at that shade-made blade. . . .
> Or else to see Ducrow with wide stride ride
> Four horses as no other man can span;
> Or in the small Olympic pit, sit split
> Laughing at Liston, while you quiz his phiz. . . .

By the fifties, every city and almost every large town had its theatre, and if not, it could see visiting companies in the Town Hall or the Corn Exchange or the Market Hall. At a later date, about 1870, England had just under two hundred theatres. London by that time had forty-four, and Liverpool nine. Manchester came next with three, and all sorts of quite small towns could support one—Bury St. Edmunds, Dewsbury, Grantham, Stamford, Leek, King's Lynn, Uxbridge, and Wigan.

But by that same date the music-hall had run ahead of the theatre. The raffish entertainment which clerks and mechanics had previously supplied among themselves was then supplied by experts, and so large a public of the unfastidious was discovered that in that year England alone had two-hundred-and-fifty-seven music-halls. London had twenty-seven; Sheffield and Liverpool ten each, and Manchester nine. Even so small a town as Dudley had seven. Leeds had six, Birmingham five, and Hanley, Grimsby, Oldham, and Rotherham, four each. Wigan had three. The names given to some of those halls were as fantastic as those given to the cinemas of to-day. At Canterbury was the Appolonian; at Oldham the Mumps, and at Birmingham the Crystal Palace and the Steam Clock (whatever that instrument was). Sheffield had a West End Palace, and Barnsley had a Wire Trellis. At Liverpool were the Casino, the Constellation, and the Parthenon. This last must have been named by somebody as learned as a film-magnate, or by somebody of sardonic humour. In many towns the hall was named, simply and fitly, the People's.

In the earliest halls of the 'forties and 'fifties, the audience, as in the original sing-songs, sat at tables and took their liquor. There were no tiers of seats as in a theatre, and no bar. Between the turns, waiters went round calling for Orders, even compelling them, and the owner looked to those orders to provide his profit. The Chairman helped in this. When the young bloods who had been granted the honour of sitting at his table sought the further honour of standing him a bottle, he always set an example by choosing champagne. The only women seen at those halls were the wives of working-class husbands or women of an equally recognisable class. The general note was that of the roystering male.

The Canterbury Music-hall in its early days

The comic songs at that time were of the coarse, clownish sort; they did not carry the leering *double-entendre* of a later time; but the males liked to imply that the entertainment took terrible forms, and that the music-hall was no place for "the ladies."

An excellent picture of a hall of the period is given in Disraeli's *Sybil*. It presents a few differences from the Harmonic Meeting of Dickens. The hall is a better kind of hall, and the entertainment is less free-and-easy and more organised. He is showing the night-life of a North Country manufacturing town, and it is no doubt typical of many another town of that time. The hall, part of a public-house, is called the Temple of the Muses. Admission is threepence, returnable when ordering a drink. The hall is on the first floor, with a door of bright green and panels gilt. Above the door the name of the hall is spelt out in letters of flaming gas. The interior of the hall is brightly decorated. It has a painted ceiling, and the walls carry panels by a local artist depicting scenes from the poets—Richard III, Mazeppa, the Lady of the Lake; Hubert with Prince Arthur, Haidee rescuing Don Juan, Jeanie Deans bowing to the Queen:

> The room was very full; some three or four hundred persons were seated in different groups at different tables, eating, drinking, talking, laughing, and even smoking, for, notwithstanding the pictures and the gilding, it was found impossible to forbid, though there were efforts to discourage, this practice in the Temple of the Muses. Nothing, however, could be more decorous than the general conduct of the company, though they consisted principally of factory people. The waiters flew about with as much agility as if they were

Leotard at the Alhambra (1861)

> serving nobles. In general the noise was great, though not disagreeable; sometimes a bell rang, and there was comparative silence, while a curtain drew up at the farther end of the room, opposite to the entrance, where there was a theatre, the stage raised at a due elevation, and adorned with side scenes, from which issued a lady in fancy-dress, who sang a favourite ballad; or a gentleman elaborately habited in a farmer's costume of the old comedy, a bob-wig, silver buttons and buckles, and blue stockings, and who favoured the company with that melancholy effusion called a comic song. Some nights there was music on the stage; a young lady in a white robe with a golden harp, and attended by a gentleman in black moustachios. . . . Otherwise the audiences of the Cat and Fiddle, we mean the Temple of the Muses, were fain to be content with four Bohemian brothers, or an equal number of Swiss sisters. The most popular amusements however were the "Thespian recitations," by amateurs or novices who wished to become professional.
>
> A sharp waiter, with a keen eye on the entering guests, immediately saluted Gerard and his friend with profuse offers of hospitality, insisting that they wanted much refreshment; that they were both very hungry and very thirsty;

56 A Gin-shop in Drury Lane, ca. 1840
From a contemporary print

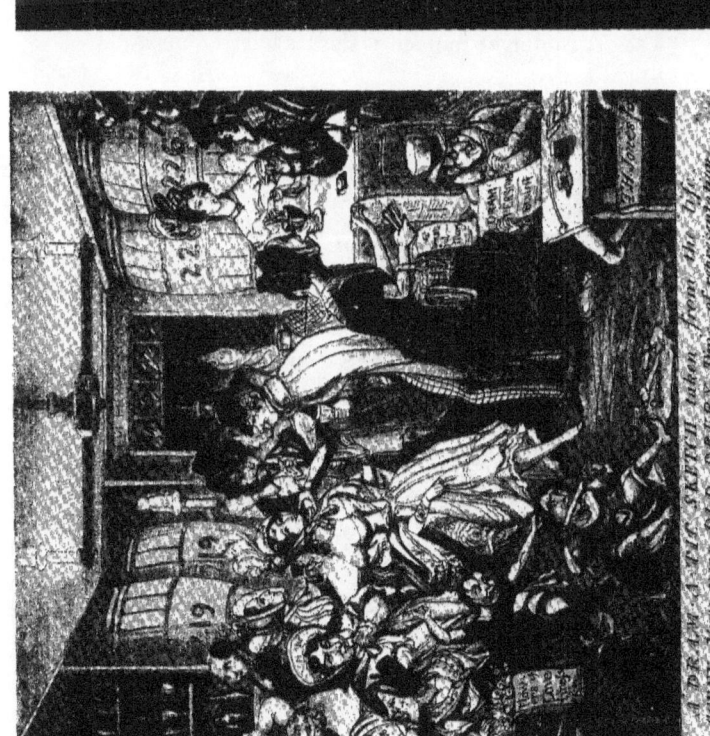

57 An Opium Den in Ratcliff, ca. 1860
From a drawing by Gustave Doré

58 A Midnight Supper in the Haymarket, 1862

59 Eight o'clock at the Opera, 1862
Both from G. A. Sala's "Twice Round the Clock"

that, if not hungry they should order something to drink that would give them an appetite; if not inclined to quaff, something to eat that would make them athirst. In the midst of these embarrassing attentions, he was pushed aside by his master with "There, go; hands wanted at the upper end; two American gentlemen from Lowell singing out for Sherry Cobbler; don't know what it is; give them our bar mixture; if they complain, say it's the Mowbray Slap-bang, and no mistake."

In London at that time, a prominent and notorious figure in the town's night life was that Renton Nicholson, mentioned earlier. He was

A Costers' Sing-song at "The Nag's Head," Clerkenwell (1865)

a purveyor of the more raffish kinds of entertainment, and was more than once in trouble. He kept, one after the other, a number of taverns, and while for a time he made a good thing out of them, he brought them all, eventually, into disrepute and decay. Some of them had been well-conducted places, but once they had been in his hands they never recovered their former estate. He had the Garrick's Head, in Bow Street; and for a time the Coal Hole, the Cyder Cellar, and Cremorne Gardens; and whatever he touched he soiled. He also edited a slightly scandalous weekly paper covering London night-life, and issued one or two pamphlets.

At the three taverns named he carried on his notorious Judge and Jury trials, at which he himself was the judge, under the style of The Lord Chief Baron. These trials were mock trials of unsavoury cases—crim. con., seduction, and so on. Plaintiff, defendant, witnesses and counsel were actors from the minor theatres, and the jury was empanelled from the supper company. The purpose of the trial was to evoke laughs by the indecent nature of the evidence. Most of the proceedings were impromptu, and some of the witnesses are said to have been remarkably adroit in their ready invention of shocking answers to the questions. The judge of course took a leading part in the game, and he too was bawdily bright in framing questions which gave excellent openings to the witnesses. These shows drew "all the town," and numbers of country visitors. All those who attended them agreed that they were a scandal and should be stopped; but they seem to have gone more than once and to have taken their friends. It was one of the "things to do." But at last authority stepped in, and did what the audience thought should be done. But they were not stopped until he had ruined with them both the Coal Hole and the Cyder Cellar.

Another of his entertainments which, according to his own account, drew all the "nobility and gentry," was given at the Garrick's Head. This was a show (admission one shilling) of *poses plastiques*—a show of frankly naked girls posed against a black curtain. This, too, shocked everybody and filled the place at every performance, and this, too, after it had filled his pockets, was put down by authority.

There is a little paper-covered book, now rather scarce, issued by him, and purporting to be edited by him. The price was five shillings, and the title-page reads: "The Swell's Night Guide to the Great Metropolis; Displaying the Saloons, the Paphian Beauties, the Chaffing Cribs, the Introducing Houses, the French Houses, etc. Edited by The Lord Chief Baron." It is one of those publications of which the nineteenth century threw up so many—half plain and half coloured; half fact and half fake. It describes all the night resorts, and the particular amusement they offered, especially his own Garrick's Head and his Cyder Cellar; and it goes on to give a list of noted women of the town, where they were to be found, and what were their habits and their expectations in the matter of reward. His advice to young men is quite Victorian in its frankness; not at all the advice that the pastors and masters of our own neurotic and scientific age would give: "Enjoy women, but let them be of the right sort. Make your heart glad with wine, but let that, too, be of the right sort, and then neither in health nor heart will you be a jot the worse. As to company, if you are told to beware of bad company, then we advise you to beware of going into any company at all." (The old cynic.) He describes his show of *poses plastiques* in luscious and leering terms, and he or his hired ghost writes in similar terms of the Royal Saloon and the Casino. The directory of the women of those places may be taken as mostly invention. The book was one of those Holywell Street things intended to appeal to the shy and unsophisticated of London and the country, who wanted to claim some knowledge of rakish life, but preferred to get it vicariously.

A sober evening entertainment that began to have a vogue in the 'fifties was the Reading, not by elocutionists but by the author himself. Thackeray drew crowded audiences to Willis's Rooms with his lectures on the English Humorists; Albert Smith packed the Egyptian Hall with his Ascent of Mont Blanc; and in 1858 Dickens, with his readings of scenes from his novels, broke all records of money-turned-away. At Liverpool his first reading drew two thousand three hundred people. In addition to tickets sold, the pay-box took two hundred pounds at the doors, and refused so much more that the one reading for which he was booked became three. From the first series of readings, Forster says, he drew for himself three hundred pounds a week.

Thackeray did very well from his lectures, and could smile at Douglas Jerrold's advice that they would go better with a piano; but he never reached that figure. Nor did anybody else. Numbers of authors, whose names convey nothing to the general reader of to-day, increased their incomes, and provided pleasant nights for the respectable, by what we now call "personal appearances" and readings from their works. But the addition was not large, and when you dig out some of those forgotten works, you wonder that the authors could have drawn even a hundred people from the domestic fireside. Authors of to-day are more modest. They still make personal appearances on platforms—especially English authors on American platforms—but I have heard of none having the courage, or perhaps one should say the effrontery, to give readings from his own works. The result anyway would be somewhat tedious. A platform reading needs drama, and our best novelists are little concerned with that. Also, few novelists or poets are capable of reading their own work with point. James Joyce, among the moderns, did read his works aloud, but not on the platform. He was wise enough to hide himself behind the mechanised protection of the gramophone.

Even if our authors did give readings, none of them, I think, would draw anything like the audiences that were drawn eighty and ninety years ago. They address evening gatherings of local Literary Societies on the Trend of the Novel or the Evolution of the Short Story, but there is no struggle at the doors, no such audience as even the forgotten Albert Smith could draw, and no such reward in money. But at that time authors were still something of a curiosity, different from the common run, and people would turn out on the wettest night to see and hear them. Apart from the Reading, which might be dramatic or comic, the serious Lecture was a popular evening diversion of the sober and sedate. It fulfilled their first demand of all recreation: it was Improving and Elevating. Coleridge and Hazlitt, somewhat earlier, had given lectures; though Coleridge, having announced a series, gave two and (characteristically) forgot to turn up for the others. Carlyle lectured on Revolutions, on Literature, on German Literature, and on Heroes; and Ruskin, and Faraday, and a number of minor men, drew popular audiences to lectures that a popular audience of to-day would hardly sit through.

Public dance-halls were becoming a prominent feature of the night-life of London and the larger towns. In the smaller towns the only public dances were those organised by a committee of townspeople and, if possible, with the patronage, if not the presence, of one or two of the County. The go-as-you-please dance-hall, or Shilling Hop, open every night, belonged to London. There was open-air dancing at Vauxhall and Cremorne, and there were the Argyll Rooms, the Holborn Casino, the Royal Saloon, Piccadilly, the Adelaide Gallery—then called Laurent's Casino, and later on to become Gatti's—and across the river the Hanover Hall. There were also a number of smaller places where you could dance for threepence. A sketch of the Argyle Rooms is given by the anonymous author of the *Life and Career of Palmer*, the poisoner, published just after his trial and conviction. The author brings it in as one of the places frequented by Palmer on his visits to London. The price of admission to the main hall and the dance floor was one shilling, and it seems that you did not have to leave your hat and coat. For an extra sixpence you could go to the gallery where there were seats:

> At the further end of the gallery, and built across the hall, you see the orchestra. In it there are fifty performers, and the gentleman conducting it, in the white choker, standing upright in the midst of them, is M. Henri Laurent, the lessee of the establishment. The band is judged by connoisseurs to be the best in London for dancers, and is highly patronised too; for not only are its strains devoted to the enlivement of the shilling public who frequent the Argyll Rooms but Majesty herself condescends to trip it to tunes composed by M. Laurent, and at every ball at Buckingham Palace his band is stationed in one of the principal rooms. A polka is going on, and looking over the balcony you will perceive that nine-tenths of the mass in the hall below is in motion. In capital tune, in the most decorous manner, the dance is carried on. You, gentle reader, from Bolton-le-Moors, might find it difficult to perform many terpsichorean feats with your hat on, and with your hand clasping the knob of a thick walking-stick, as well as your partner's digits; but the habitué of the Argyll scorns such slight matters, and can perform his favourite steps even when encumbered with the thickest poncho

or the stoutest umbrella. You will perceive that there are several masters of the ceremonies, distinguishable by their levee evening dress, and by the gaudy rosettes on their coats, and that the slightest impropriety is instantly repressed. . . . Here, in the corner of the gallery, you perceive a buffet for refreshments, but if you are not particularly thirsty, we would caution you to wait until you retire, as cheapness is not an item that has been overlooked by the proprietor in his catering. And now for the company; here, in this gallery, where the more select are supposed to congregate, we have seen peers of the realm, officers of the highest rank in the army and navy, leading members of the House of Commons, aye, and judges of the land!

The gallery company was not there to dance; merely to look on and observe how the "common" people—shop-boys, clerks, milliner's girls, sempstresses—amused themselves at night; and to be themselves amused by the antics and capers of some who thought they were dancing. Perhaps to pick up a supper companion. When they danced in public they went to the *bals masqués* at the Lyceum, where the conductor was Jullien, who, at the same house, gave the first London promenade concerts; or to Willis's Rooms or similar semi-private places.

The dancing at Cremorne seems to have been of the style of that at the Argyle Rooms, but the dancers were not so orderly. In 1857 the place was indicted as a nuisance because of the hullabaloo that went on after midnight, the shouting and singing, and disputing of cab fares, and sometimes fights. There was much controversy for and against closing the Gardens at eleven o'clock, but the summons, when heard, was dismissed. *Punch* entered on the side of the Gardens, and objected to any attempt to compel the closing of the Gardens at an earlier hour than the theatres. At the same time it made a solemnly-waggish objection to late hours. Noise was perhaps made in the Gardens after midnight, but so it was outside some great houses in fashionable squares after a ball. Anyway, respectable people, it implied, would not be in the Gardens after midnight, and should not be prevented from enjoying an evening there because of the behaviour at later hours of a rowdy few. Decent people, it said, walked off before to-morrow walked in. People with the duties of life to observe—it excluded "Swells and Ministers and other useless beings"—must be up at eight o'clock and at work by ten. Nobody with work to do could want to be at a place of amusement after midnight. Leaving the Gardens at that hour, and allowing for the journey home, and a final cigar, he would be in bed by one o'clock, and fit to rise at eight. "Therefore, we have nothing to say to anybody who stays at Cremorne, or anywhere else, at unseemly hours, except that he ought to be ashamed of himself."

If that is so, then thousands of people in mid-Victorian times should have been going about bowed with shame. Unseemly hours were kept by all sorts of people; those with work to do and those with none. And those who had things to do somehow managed to do them without the seven hours sleep which *Punch* considered necessary. Many young men, and some not so young, got home at three or four, sometimes with the milk, yet managed to be at their place of business at ten. It was an age of two polar ways of life; either a respectability almost Quakerish or the flagrant looseness of Champagne Charlie. There was, of course, as there always is, a mid-way, which enjoyed a little of each, but the memoirs of those who lived their youth in that time show that the insistent notes were imposed by the two extremes. From one man's Recollections you gather that it was an age of piety, plain living, and industry. Take up another volume, and you gather that life was all bubbly, rickety-rackety, rowdy-dowdy; with no going home at all, not even at morning.

In the sixties the song of *Champagne Charlie* went all over England, and became a favourite with the young men of the most rural towns. It even penetrated to Suffolk. Fitzgerald, in one of his letters, mentions the haunting effect of its polka-time air, and how every wandering musician and singer brought it to the villages. But the song was only a tardy expression of a spirit that had been abroad for some years in both town and country—a sort of aftermath of Corinthianism. The novels of Surtees present a good picture of the social life of the countryside in the Early Victorian years, and though they were written before that song appeared, we meet in most of them one or two characters of the type crystallised in the song. There are Sir Harry Scattercash and his friends in *Mr. Sponge's Sporting Tour*; Mr. Waffles and Mr. Pacey in the same book; Jasper Goldspink in *Plain or Ringlets?* and Cuddy Flintoff in *Ask Mamma*. All of them dashers and flashers, or thinking they are.

The more sober country nights, as shown by Surtees, were those of Hunt balls, fancy-dress balls, and receptions in the Assembly Rooms. There were, of course, concerts and lectures, though the lectures were not perhaps so extravagant as the "Sporting Lectors" of Jorrocks at Handley Cross, which some writers on Surtees have identified with Tunbridge Wells. And when there was nothing else, there were long dinners at each other's houses, and after dinner, long sittings by the men round the horseshoe table, with anchovy toasts and devilled biscuits, and no inclination at all to join the ladies.

The most elegant and lavish party described in the novels is that given by the penniless Lucy Glitters when sharing Beldon Hall with

Facey Romford. It began at nine, and went on till morning. Half the county was invited, and Lucy ordered from the leading London caterer a complete champagne supper for about a hundred guests, with the necessary waiters, and a first-class orchestra for the ball-room. She also ordered exquisite evening gowns for herself and her friend, liveries for the groom and the gardener and the game-keeper, who were brought in as indoor servants, and muslin dresses for the two maids. None of this, of course, was to be paid for; she merely took advantage of the effect of coronetted note-paper on London tradespeople. The supper-table, supervised by the caterer's men, was decorated at the top with a large sugar replica of the Royal Arms, at the middle with a symbol of India—a large sugar elephant—and at the bottom with a barley-sugar pagoda, surrounded by boxes of crackers. Down its centre ran a line of turkeys, chickens, hams, tongues, jellies, creams and custards, boar's-head, plovers' eggs, pigeon-pies, lobster salads, tipsy-cake, pineapples and cheesecakes.

But Lucy, a Londoner, knowing little of party-giving in the country, had made no arrangements for the carriages and horses and coachmen of her guests. In London, carriages set down, went away, and came back at the hour of breaking-up. But country dinners often meant a journey of many miles for some of the guests, and the host always arranged rough stabling for the horses and cover for the carriages, and supper in the servants' hall for the coachmen. None of this was done at Beldon Hall; carriages and coachmen stood out in the frosty drive until one or two of the bolder spirits lost patience. After demanding the customary refreshment, and learning from the servants that no orders had been given, a raiding party went into the supper room, after dancing had begun, and carried off hams, tongues, chickens, bottles of champagne, the sugar elephant, and anything they could get hold of. The night ended with the wreck of the supper-table, and a fight in the hall between one of the coachmen and the gamekeeper-butler.

A passing remark in one of the Surtees novels provides a link between those times and our own. When arranging a dinner or ball, considerate hosts and hostesses, knowing that many of their guests had to come long distances, tried to avoid nights of complete darkness. They made their arrangements, as we do in this present year, for nights of full moon. But they enjoyed the night without the trepidation that we know.

The dance hall flourished everywhere. The lowest and roughest halls were found in the ports, near the docks. They were usually only the basements of taverns, and there was no admission charge. James

Greenwood, in one of his London books, gives a vivid description of night-life in Ratcliff Highway about 1870. At that time the street was lined with taverns, and dance and singing rooms. The chief of these were Paddy's Goose, the Prussian Flag, and the Pickled Herring, where all the women from Tiger Bay, a block of three streets so-called from its inhabitants, gathered to pick up the sailors and get them tight enough to be easily robbed. The dancing-room of the Prussian Flag, as Greenwood describes it, was a long room with a resplendent bar at one end, and at the other the "orchestra"—four street musicians, who wore their hats or caps, and smoked clay pipes between the items. The women, before dancing, removed their hats and hung them on a row of hooks. All were dressed in silk or satin, with bare arms and shoulders, and all of them were hard-faced and hard-voiced. The men, most of whom were drunk, were seafaring men of all countries—Italians, Germans, African negroes, Americans, Britons, and men from the East, brown, copper-coloured, and yellow. Some of them danced in sea-boots; some of them, for greater agility, removed coat and waistcoat. But everything was orderly. Four hefty young bruisers attended to that. They moved about the room, coatless, with shirt-sleeves rolled back, showing their biceps. They acted as waiters, but their real job was to keep order, and to see that no robbery or fight happened on the premises. What happened off the premises was no concern of theirs. They would stop two girls from trying to rob a drunken sailor, and would put all three out in the street. They knew that the job would be done there, but they were not interested in the sailor; only in preserving the "good name" of the house.

While Greenwood was there, one of the girls, whose escort, a negro, was not spending enough, went for him and cut his lip. The other negroes joined in, to get him away from her, but before the fight could develop, the four waiters were on them, and in a minute or so, the whole party was outside and the waiters calmly came back and went on serving.

In the Highway at that time a number of Chinese had their homes, and many of them kept opium rooms. One of them, known as Johnson's, was put into literature by Dickens. He described it in *Edwin Drood* as the house frequented by John Jasper for his secret indulgences. Greenwood went to it some time later, and Blanchard Jerrold. Their descriptions, when set with that given by Dickens, show that his observation was as exact as always, and that he used no fanciful exaggeration.

Greenwood's excursions into queer sides of night-life made him, in the early 'seventies, the centre of a sensation. He was writing then for

60 After Dinner in an Early Victorian Drawing-room
From a drawing by Eugène Lami

61 An Evening at Cremorne in the 'Sixties

62 Members of the Audience, 1874

63 A Game of Whist, 1865

the *Daily Telegraph*, and one of his excursions took him to the Potteries. There, one night, he managed to be present at a private sporting event which, when he described it, called forth a stream of protests and expressions of disgust. But the Press of the Potteries met the protests with protests of their own. They did not charge James Greenwood with fanciful exaggeration. They, and numbers of local people, charged him with fantastic invention. They implied that either he was confusing a bad dream with reality, or he had "made it up." No such sporting event, they were sure, had ever happened in their district. They called upon him for proof; asked him to bring forward anybody who was present at the event, and could confirm his story. He tried to, but he couldn't. He had been taken by two labourers whom he had met in a bar; but when he tried to locate those men, or the principal of the affair, they had vanished. All those of whom he could give any description had vanished; and for a long time he rested under the imputation of writing false news. But he persisted that the thing had happened exactly as he described and in the place named.

The *Telegraph* itself then took up the matter, and he and the editor spent weeks and months in defending his integrity as a journalist and in travelling about the Potteries, trying to find somebody who would confirm him.

The particular sporting event was a fight between a muscular dwarf and a savage bull-dog. It took place late at night in the cellar of a house just outside Hanley. In the middle of the cellar a ring had been made, strewn with sawdust and enclosed by ropes and posts. The dog and the dwarf were each tethered to opposite posts by a chain which, at its full extent, brought them just within reach of each other. The man fought on his knees, and was allowed to use only his fists. About fifty sportsmen were present, some labourers and some "swells." The details of the fight are too unpleasant to quote; it ended, after the dwarf had been badly mauled, in his knocking the dog out.

The Man-and-Dog-Fight mystery occupied columns of the Press of London and of many other parts than the Potteries. The *Telegraph* reached the point of offering a hundred pounds reward to anybody who would produce, or enable them to find, the dwarf or his backers. Greenwood and Le Sage were brought into touch with several men who, in confidence, practically admitted that such a fight had taken place, and who knew where the dwarf was to be found. But there was so much secrecy, so many conditions, so much talk about the number of men who had to be "squared" before they would produce the dwarf, so many men who knew a friend of his who saw him every day, but had forgotten the friend's name and address, that finally the mystery became, in the newspaper sense, "cold," and was no more heard of.

But there are other records that in the Potteries and the Black Country and the North, many illegal sporting events took place at night. None so brutal and horrible as the Man-and-Dog, perhaps; but many a main of cocks was fought in those districts, and dog-fights were frequent events. They happened in London too. Even bear-baiting and badger-baiting could be seen at some secret places by those who were guaranteed "safe." Compared with the people whose tastes in entertainment ran to that kind of thing, the Champagne Charlies were harmless and decent.

Music-halls, in the 'seventies and 'eighties, were at their peak of popularity, and their number continued to grow. In their new form of Theatres of Variety they were the favourite evening entertainment of the people. The full story of them, from their dim beginnings up to the present, has been delightfully told by Willson Disher in his *Winkles and Champagne*, a contribution to social history and to folk-lore. But, like all the amusements of the ordinary people, they came in for fierce criticism. There were those who could see nothing in them, and thought them only a substitute for entertainment for illiterate boys. And there were those who could see quite a lot in them; they could even see Satan. They were places where the workers wasted their time and their money, when they should have been at home resting in their masters' interest for the next day's labour. The Varieties they offered were varieties of temptation. Sin stalked on the stage, and flaunted itself among the young men of the audience, in the guise of jest and jollity. The morbid people who always attack popular amusement even suggested that they were not only places where Thoughtless Youth might be Led Astray, but that they were set up for that purpose. There were calls for their suppression.

Apart from these foolish and intemperate attacks, they were regarded generally with contempt, even by some of those who patronised them. Actors and actresses were accepted, or at least tolerated, but music-hall people were regarded—to a large extent justly—as belonging to an altogether lower class, if not the gutter. A writer in a monthly magazine of the time, *London Society*, writing wistfully of the old clowns and harlequinades, wrote very sharply of music-hall people:

> The present generation is acquainted with a class of mummers and drolls which did not exist a quarter of a century ago. This class includes nigger serenaders and the so-called comic singers at the music-halls. The niggers, relying to a great extent upon music of a popular and catching kind, are

universally popular; and their grotesque antics are often exceedingly amusing. . . . Of the general run of comic singers at the music-halls the less said the better. They cannot sing; they are vulgar, ignorant, and offensive; and their songs are gross and indecent, without one redeeming touch of wit or humour. When the theatrical monopoly—that last dirty rag of protection—has been broken up, and anyone will be at liberty to act plays where he chooses, under the ordinary regulations for the preservation of public order, these blatant fellows will be sent back to their proper occupation, the sweeping out of shops and the scouring of pewter pots.

But there was no end to the criticism of and interference with the nights of the people. When the people chose to spend their nights at the music-hall, they were frivolous. When they attended to this criticism, and mended their ways by spending serious nights at Debating Societies, again they were wrong. They were attacked then for taking in political poison by listening to "clap-trap at Spouting Clubs." Working-men's clubs and those open Debating Societies, where "gents visiting the room are invited to take part in the discussions," were seen as forcing-beds of revolution and the overthrow of the Constitution. Why couldn't the young men go to a good concert? The young men listened again, and again mended their ways. They went in large numbers to popular concerts, at a shilling admission. And when they did this, the same paper that had urged them to do it, spoke sneeringly of the concerts as patronised by an audience of "gents."

The majority, though, took no notice of criticism. They went on patronising the halls, and the halls became bigger and bigger, and brighter and brighter, and paid larger and larger salaries to their stars. But with all their brilliance they were still rather out of it. Not until the twentieth century did they become places where everybody could be seen. Through the latter years of the nineteenth century they were either places for the ordinary people, or, in the case of the huge West End houses—the Alhambra, Empire, and Palace—where ballet was the main attraction, they were the night-haunts of the young bloods of the universities, the old dogs from the clubs, and prostitutes who made their Promenades their rendezvous. Through the 'eighties and 'nineties, Boat Race Night at the Empire or the Alhambra was a saturnalia of smashed hats, black eyes, and broken heads—a sort of Donnybrook Fair in white ties.

The very respectable kept away from them. There were for them other entertainments which could bring no embarrassment to demure eyes. There were in London the Moore and Burgess Minstrels at St. James's Hall; the Magic and Mystery entertainments at Egyptian Hall; the German-Reed entertainments; and for the poorer people there were the Penny Readings and the Spelling Bees. Most of those means of killing an evening have passed away. The Magic and Mystery entertainment alone remains. A few years ago the B.B.C. revived the rather tedious Spelling Bee over the radio, without, I believe, a much delighted reception. The Penny Reading—a series of "recitations" given in Parish Halls, admission one penny—died young. Its purpose apparently was to draw the working people from the public-house and the music-hall. From what one can learn of it, its prospects of success were poor.

The Minstrels, a polished entertainment of its kind, would also have little appeal to-day. In one advertisement they claim to have played ten times a week at the St. James's Hall for a continuous season of eleven years, without missing "one lawful day"; and they went on much longer than that. They passed when certain music-halls, under Moss and Stoll, offered entertainment for the family, with polite piano entertainers and discreet clowns and musical ensembles on drawing-room sets. As for the German-Reed entertainments, from what I heard of them in my youth from my elders, anybody of to-day, child or adult, dragged to a reproduction of one of them, would either go to sleep or scream. But they had a justification which was shown by their success. They offered something on the hither side of the theatre and the music-hall for those whose scruples kept them away from such places. They offered a thoroughly "refined" entertainment, forgetting perhaps the sense of the word, and that you can refine a thing until you have nothing left.

From the 'seventies onward, dining in public restaurants, and even late suppers, became possible for women; not only for the fast but for women of position. It was a little "daring," but it was done. It was said that the old bohemian Evans' Supper Room committed suicide when it opened a room where men could entertain women guests. Certainly something went wrong, and it died; but by that time there were several restaurants which were purely restaurants, without any atmosphere of hilarity or song or masculine good fellowship. One of these was the Maison Dorée. An article in a weekly paper of 1871, describing the "night out" of a young girl, mentions it as one of "the" places. The Captain takes his fiancée and her friend there for "a little feed." With the coffee the girls venture to smoke a Turkish cigarette, and after dinner the Captain takes them in a cab to some corner right off the earth, where they are set down at a sort of theatre, at which the Captain has a box, and where they see a performance of an Offenbach operetta. They discover later that they have been to the Philharmonic at Islington.

Another periodical of the same year has a reference to the new and strange fashion which permitted "ladies" to take after-theatre suppers in restaurants. A very County woman asks her military son to take her somewhere for supper—some place where a woman can go with propriety. The answer is—where, at that hour of the night, could they go without impropriety? But then he remembers that in the changed times women of the highest rank may go almost anywhere without impropriety. He suggests a place near Haymarket—Wilcocks's—with a warning that it will have mixed company; "actresses and that sort of thing"; but immediately adds that everybody goes to Wilcocks's— Everybody—the Marchioness of —— and Lady —— were there the other night, and without escort. So they go, and take a "light" supper —fried kidneys, sausages, cold duck, fried potatoes, cherry tart and cream, Stilton, and champagne. One of the party asks the County woman whether it was quite right for her son to have brought them there; some of the "persons" do not look "correct." With a slight shudder at the rude force of democracy, the County woman answers: "In the present day, my dear, it is quite impossible to say who is correct and who is incorrect. There used to be a costume for the members of each world, but fashion has changed; class trenches upon class more and more, and we must go with the times." Remarks follow—that a few years ago no "lady" would have dreamt of taking supper, or any meal, at a public place; yet in 1871 some of the *best* people were doing it. Well-well. . . .

The restaurants and night-houses actually in Haymarket itself were another matter. "Ladies" were not seen at the Blue Posts, or Barron's Oyster Rooms or the Burmese, or the Piccadilly Saloon. Haymarket at that time was regarded by social students as a blot on London; an abomination; a cesspool of midnight corruption; a street of infamy. The terms are taken from contemporary writers, many of whom were familiar with it and not wholly as social students. It is not easy to discover in what the infamy consisted. It never is. The fact is merely stated, with a supplementary murmur that the details are unfit for publication. One is left to draw inferences. But from a point here and a point there it appears that it was lit up from end to end all night, and that almost every building was an all-night restaurant for loose company, or a gaming-room, or a bath-house, or an expensive bordel. From midnight to dawn it was roaring with disorder. Fights were frequent. Much money was spent or lost there, and more champagne bottles emptied than in any other street.

One gathers, in short, that in Haymarket of those years people did what nobody, however rich, can do to-day. They did as they pleased. The result, judging from Victorian memoirs with their records of early deaths and early ruin, seems to show that licence is as useful a corrective as repression. Under licence, the fools exterminated themselves and troubled the world no more. Under the twentieth-century control of our daily and nightly hours, they still hang about and impede the world.

Until a new licensing law of the 'seventies fixed a uniform closing-hour of 12.30 a.m., most West End restaurants were open half the night. Among them were the Café Riche at the top of Haymarket; Rouget's, back of Leicester Square; Meurigy's, in Lower Regent Street; the Café Regence, in Windmill Street; and our own Café Royal. Their night really began at midnight, but it was not all rowdiness. Most of them were well-conducted places, frequented by quiet people. If the anonymous author of *London in the Sixties* may be trusted, the rowdiness was made chiefly by Army officers and undergraduates, and they had restaurants and night-houses of their own in which to loose their loutishness. Some of the behaviour he records can hardly be believed by modern readers; no Army officer of to-day, in his most hilarious midnight moments, would sink to such ugly nonsense. But in those days many officers were the more useless members of old families, who bought commissions, served for a year or two, and then sold out of a career for which they were never fitted.

The nights of champagne and brandy which the anonymous author describes naturally led to bad mornings, and he mentions the kind of afternoon "breakfast" with which some of his friends tried to pull themselves together—mackerel bones fried in gin; caviare on cayenne toast; devilled biscuits; and a livener whose pungency is hinted by its popular name, Fixed Bayonets. Hotels of to-day are seldom asked for so drastic a breakfast, though I did, not long ago, encounter two cases of orders for inhuman refreshment. I was in the cocktail bar of a Strand hotel when an elderly man came to the counter and ordered a double brandy, and asked the bar-tender to shake in a few drops of Tobasco sauce. He caught my eye as he gave the order, and explained: "Just so that I can *taste* it." The second case I found at the grill-room bar of a Regent Street restaurant. Again he was elderly, and he asked for an absinthe. He was told that they did not serve absinthe. He asked what they meant—there was the bottle on the shelf. Yes; but that was only used for adding a spot or two to cocktails; they did not serve "an" absinthe. He asked how much they served in cocktails, and was told—just a shake or so; four or five drops. He held out his hand, cupped, and said: "Give me in my hand as much as you put in a cocktail." The bar-tender gave the bottle a shake or so and made a small pool in the hand, and the man put his nose to his hand and took it up as one takes snuff. It was like meeting the ghost of Jack Mytton.

While supper-parties were given in public by many of the more alert, night-life among the sedate middle-class, even as late as the 'eighties, was mainly domestic. Wholesale communal night-life did not become a fashion until the twentieth-century era of flats and cars, and the decay of large houses, and the servant shortage. Woman's place was still the home, in spite of the movement for emancipation, and the old-fashioned, who were not necessarily themselves old, did not feel that they had entertained their friends unless they had done it at their own table and in their own drawing-room. But getting through the evening was often a problem, and many articles and books were published by presumed experts on How to Do It. One of the articles of the time states the problem without offering very much in the way of meeting it:

> The employment of the interval between dinner and going to bed is a problem which everybody solves according to his own lights and opportunities. Some people, living in the country, dine at seven, and retire to rest at ten, which is like cutting the Gordian knot instead of untying it. In town, on the contrary, society who congregate by night will dine a little earlier than usual, and prolong their evening into morning. Going to the theatre, and such-like, is so obvious, self-suggestive, and matter-of-fact a way of disposing of your after-dinner hours, that it is needless to say anything further about it. Whether you go for the sake of the performance, like the virtuoso, or of the audience, like the fop and the coquette, your amusement is provided ready-made; your evening, exactly like your dinner, is prepared for you by other heads and hands; you simply defray the cost thereof, and then have only to sit still and be entertained without thought of others; or, if you prefer it, fall asleep....
> Evening parties present the grand difficulty of how to occupy the time. It requires great tact and talent on the part of the master or mistress of the house to keep up pleasant conversation in a small coterie. Hence the expediency, sometimes the necessity, of introducing cards. Another method of amusing your friends is to get together twice as many people as your house will hold. The crush in your rooms, the crowd on your staircase, the impossibility of getting in, and the equal impossibility of getting out again, afford continual entertainment which never flags until your visitors take their final flight.

That form of hospitality, or practical joke, is used by many hosts and hostesses to-day. That it was general in the 'seventies and 'eighties is shown by a number of Du Maurier's drawings of social jams and of salons with no empty space save above the heads of the company. Sitting on the floor was not then correct, and as there never were enough chairs, exhausted guests went either limp-kneed and jelly-backed, or rigid with cramp.

But in the late 'eighties, by the example of the then Prince of Wales, public entertaining became more general. By that time Ritz had opened the Savoy and the Carlton, with Escoffier as chef. Their restaurants were the first to offer music, not in the dining-room itself but in the lounge or palm-court, where coffee was taken. There was also the Berkeley, with Francatelli as chef. And the old-established Verrey's, in Regent Street, was another place where the mixed dinner-party was seen. One of the Prince's favourite places was the Carlton, where he often dined and afterwards listened to the music; and where the Prince went of course everybody went. At least, they went where he openly went. Some of them would no doubt have hesitated to go to some of the places he visited incognito.

Through the 'sixties and 'seventies he had set the pace of London's night-life, and had been interested in all sides of life, as a prince should be. Social memoirs of the period make guarded references to this, and one or two periodicals make open references. One meets stories of a Haroun-al-Raschid kind about a Highly-placed Personage, with coat collar turned up and hat pulled down, being seen in many queer places. Or stories of an Important Figure being conducted in disguise to some place where the life was rather more elemental than the life of Balmoral or Osborne. In that long period between full manhood and participation in affairs, his night-wanderings seem to have belied the Chinese proverb which says that it is the height of folly to seek the person of the sacred Emperor in the common tea-houses. It was just in the equivalent places of London that the official bodyguard were sometimes able to find him, after he had contrived to lose them.

He is said to have been a frequent visitor to the music-halls, even the over-the-water hall, the Canterbury. The bar of the Canterbury was a sort of midnight Finish for the stars of the halls. Most of them lived on the South side, and it was a custom among them, when their evening's work was done, to call at the Canterbury for a "final." The bar was one of the sights of those times. At midnight "everybody" was there; all those whose names make the history of the halls. Another sight was the road outside, where the crowd waited to see them, and where their hired conveyances stood in a long line—broughams, gaudy barouches, phaetons, landaus, down to the humble hansom and four-wheeler.

Every London district then had its hall, and it seems that the Prince at one time or another visited most of them. There were halls in what seem to us of to-day incongruous places. Knightsbridge had a hall. There was a hall in Marylebone High Street. There was one at Kensington. It was the boom period for the music-hall, but the art of the halls was still coldly regarded by the people of the theatre. They were

The Canterbury in 1890

then separate worlds, and their people seldom mixed. Actors and actresses were seen in drawing-rooms, but music-hall people, as I said earlier, were almost outcasts. An advertisement in an old music-hall paper rather points this. Leeds had both theatres and music-halls, but the companies touring them seem to have kept apart, and a certain tavern offers a welcome to music-hall people and invites them to come in and be among friends: "Fred French—At Home—Grantham Arms. Social Gatherings Every Sunday Evening. London, Provincial, and Continental Papers Kept." Old actors spoke of the theatre as "the legitimate," leaving an implication that the people of the halls were what the taxi-driver implied when he had driven a young man from Hampstead to the Bachelors' Club, and received twopence over the fare—"I got a proper tip yesterday when I drove yer father here."

"Going it at the Canterbury," 1892
From a drawing by L. Raven Hill

The London night of that time had an orchestration quite different from that of our time. Our peace-time nights went to the accompaniment of hum and glow. Those other nights were nights of glitter and jingle. They were lit by brilliance rather than volume, and their festive noise was that of hoofs and harness bells. The hansom cab and the Inverness cape were the essential elements and expression of a period. They made a fit match, and could not rightly live apart. The Inverness cape would not suit the taxi or the Rolls, and modern fashions would look wooden against the frivolous and fragile hansom. The Inverness cape also was a fit companion to the antics that went with those nights. A phrase of the time for a night out was "going on the bat," and the flashing and flapping of the cape as young men swung in and out of the St. James's Bar, the Criterion Long Bar, or the Blue Posts in Cork Street, or wrestled with policemen, certainly gave an illusion of the wings of the night-bird. As to the antics of their owners, an elderly friend summed up for me the London nights of his youth, in a brief sentence—Wherever you saw a man of your own age in evening rig, you either knocked his Gibus off or stood him a drink; sometimes both.

Among poets and artists, the form for an intellectual evening was to go to the Empire or Alhambra, and see the ballet; then to one of the bars; and to finish the night in a cabmen's shelter with eggs-and-bacon. It was one of the affectations of an age of affectations, like slumming. Favourite shelters were that near the Langham Hotel, that about midway down Piccadilly, and one near the Gaiety Bar. Intellectuals "took up" the music-hall, as they have taken up the films, coming a little late, as they always do, to discover what the ordinary people had discovered years ago. There were essays on the music-hall and poems on the music-hall. The title of one of John Davidson's volumes of verse was *In a Music Hall*, and poems on the same theme are scattered in the volumes of Mr. Arthur Symons and one or two others of the period. They made a cult of it, and unhappily, as always happens when anything becomes a cult, they made it self-conscious and so hastened its end.

Years ago Mr. George Morrow, in a mood of perhaps unconscious prophecy, did a *Punch* picture on the intentionally extravagant idea of a night in the future with the Folk-Lore Society. It showed the earnest students sitting gravely in a circle while a music-hall comedian of the red-nose-baggy-trousers-battered-hat-and-umbrella type gives a recital from his repertoire of songs about cheese, kippers, tripe, and mothers-in-law. But, like so many of *Punch's* extravagant glimpses into the future, it was inspired. It, or something like it, very nearly happened. You may remember that when Harry Champion, a comedian of the people, made an appearance in a West End revue with his *Any Old Iron?* he eclipsed all the modern dry, smart comedy, and was the hit of the evening, and was everywhere discussed as a superb comic. He had for years been singing that song and others like it in ordinary music-halls, to the delight of his audiences; yet if you had mentioned his name in a drawing-room your friends would either have wondered what you were talking about, or, if you had explained, would have wondered that you could have such low tastes. And then, in a few weeks, *Any Old Iron?* was known and talked of in quite serious circles, and will no doubt pass into history, like *Champagne Charlie* and *Villikins and his*

Dinah. But at the time he revived it, the music-halls in which it was born, the real music-halls, were gone. He was giving us, in accord with George Morrow's prophetic picture, something out of folk-lore.

Towards the end of the nineteenth century London had three centres of night-life, which set a sort of standard of "gaiety" for provincial towns and seaside resorts—the Strand, Leicester Square, and Piccadilly Circus. Each of them was celebrated in contemporary song—"Strolling down the Strand, that's where I do the grand" . . . "Leicester Square, I was there, Along with Polly, awfully jolly" . . . "The Piccadilly Johnny, with a window in his eye." They were on fire every night with young men and old boys from the Gardenia Club, the Alsatian, and other night-resorts. Men of the C Division on night duty had an arduous job. In the years before the war we had a little annual excitement in West End streets on Boat Race nights, but the kind of Boat Race night this generation knows is just a reproduction of almost *any* night of the 'eighties and 'nineties. When the noctambulists of those years really let go—when they did have a Boat Race Night or a St. Patrick's Night or a New Year's Eve round St. Paul's—they made, as I said earlier, a saturnalia of a kind that the young have never seen. Present members of the C Division may have heard from their seniors about those Boat Race nights, and may be glad they were not serving at that time; or perhaps regretful. Tastes differ. The Circus then was very much a circus; clowns were everywhere, and at several points the harlequinade was played with real policemen. The scene in the Square was like an insane ballet danced by puppets. Arrests and rescues were part of the ballet. In memoirs and recollections of the period one finds many a reference to sprints down Piccadilly and hot-foot pursuits. Record time seems often to have been made for the quarter-mile by both offender and officer. It usually ended in a tie and an ungainly march to Vine Street. When, in 1939, that station was closed, I made the suggestion that it should be preserved as one of London's Historic Monuments—remembering the number of distinguished men who, in their youth, have spent a night there.

The Strand at that time was the centre of the theatre world, and it had many more restaurants than now. It was commonly said, indeed, that when any building in the Strand became vacant it was at once taken and opened as an oyster room, a smart restaurant, or a chop-and-sausage place. It was not the sedate business street it is to-day; its business was pleasure, and its nights, when its "iron lilies" were aflame, and the theatres were emptying and the restaurants filling, were nights of carnival taken with a nonchalance that London has not known for

64 The Empire Promenade, 1892

65 Behind the Scenes, 1889

66 An Evening Reception
From a "Punch" drawing by George du Maurier

67 Mounting the Stairs
From a "Punch" drawing by George du Maurier

nearly thirty years. Its crowd was not of the fashionable world; that world only passed through it from home to theatre and back. It was mainly a street of actors, poets, artists, journalists, actresses, and chorus ladies and their young-men attendants. The stage-door of the lighter theatre was then quite an institution. Every night at every door was a line of broughams and hansoms, and clustered round the door were numbers of opera-hatted young men, of rather vacuous faces, holding shower bouquets and other tributes. As one after another of the ladies came out, the favoured one would carry her off to supper at one of the right places—Scott's, Romano's, the Savoy, the Cavour, the Globe, or the Chatham. Chorus ladies of that time differed from the hard-working, quiet girls of to-day. Most of them then could somehow afford to keep a brougham and a maid and a finely-furnished flat. They were the divinities of their age, and whatever they wanted, somebody seems to have provided.

Many glimpses of the looser night-life of the 'nineties may be caught in the books of Arthur Binstead—those rambling, inconsequent, and very entertaining things, *Gal's Gossip, More Gal's Gossip, Pitcher in Paradise, A Pink 'Un and a Pelican,* etc. They are anecdotal books, the anecdotes centring chiefly on the *Sporting Times* group, Romano's bar, and Phil May. Phil May's own nights make a sort of epitome of the period. Nights at the National Sporting Club, nights at Romano's, nights at the Pelican Club, the Eccentric, the Savage. One of the stories turns on Phil May's winning some money (about forty pounds) on a boxing-match at the National Sporting Club. Being Phil May, he had to spend it. He invited a group of friends to supper at Romano's. But the guests hadn't much appetite, and even with the fine wines he ordered he found he wasn't spending fast enough. So he ordered a fresh fruit salad, with liqueur dressing. The time was mid-winter, and the *maître d'hôtel* murmured to him that at that season a real fresh-fruit salad—strawberries, raspberries, apricots, melon, pine-apple, peaches—would mean a very high price. Phil May blew the question away. "Bring a fresh fruit salad." There was some quick scampering around Covent Garden market, and after some delay a vast silver bowl of summer fruits dressed with a bottle of maraschino appeared. Supper finished with coffee, cigars, and *fine champagne,* and Phil May called for the bill. When it came he threw it down with disgust. Even with the fruit salad he hadn't achieved his object. It was only about thirty-two pounds.

There was not much hilarity about Phil May's nights. They were, in one sense, very sober nights, however drunk he might be. There is a story of his being one night with a group who had just left Romano's. One of them somehow had got hold of a surveyor's steel tape measure, and was playing with it. As they were parting at Charing Cross, Phil May looked at it, then looked at the man who had it, and said "Stand where you are." He took one end of it, and walked across the road,

The Trocadero Bar
From a drawing by Phil May

pulling it out behind him. On the other side he stooped down, made a careful measurement, and brought out a note-book. The police held up the traffic. The man who had the measure saw the idea, and he too stooped down, and held the thing taut. Phil May then cried "Come on!" and they crossed to the top of Northumberland Avenue. Phil May went to the opposite side, and again the traffic was held up, and the same business gone through. Then to the top of Whitehall, where it was repeated, and traffic into and out of Whitehall was stopped. Phil May then paced to the centre of the road, and after consulting his note-book, marked out a large square in chalk. He then called to his friend to wind-in the measure, thanked the constables for their help, gravely joined his friend, and walked away.

Another night, when he was with a similar group, they passed a point where part of the road was up. The men had left their tools on the spot, enclosed in the usual little red railings. Phil May said nothing. He looked at these things and looked at his friends. Without a word each man picked up railings or tools, and walked off, led by Phil May. He led them to one of the quiet Strand streets—Surrey or Norfolk Street—and, in the middle of the road, set up a section of the railing. Then, with pick-axes, they went to work. When the exercise had produced a useful sweat, and a good section of the road was "up," Time was called, they downed tools, and went back to Romano's.

Bohemian life was often like that; not all rowdiness; sometimes demurely playful. There was a little night-occasion at Cambridge about that time, arranged by a well-known practical joker, which one would have liked to assist at. The thing was all over in an hour, but the arranging occupied some months. The joker arrived in Cambridge, and, step by step, managed somehow to make the acquaintance of a Mr. Higginbotham, a Mr. Longbotham, a Mr. Sidebotham, a Mr. Rowbotham, a Mr. Bottome, and a Mr. Penbotham. When, at last, he knew them all, he invited each of them to dine with him at one of the Cambridge hotels. On the night, and at the time appointed, the six men turned up. None of them knew each other, but they found they were all guests of the same man, and they were shown into a reception room where a waiter handed round aperitifs. After some twenty minutes, the head-waiter brought a message to the company that a telegram had just arrived from the host, saying that there had been a slight accident on the railway, and he was afraid he would be much delayed in joining them. It was his wish that dinner should be served without waiting for him.

He didn't turn up at all. The guests were shown into a private dining-room, and then the waiters set before each guest one dish under a silver cover. When they lifted their covers they found that each of them had a large, nicely-grilled *rump* steak.

The Café Royal, in the 'nineties, was so recognised a centre for nightly gatherings of art and letters, and so identified with the new movements of the time, that it was almost a symbol of them. It was the only real café, on the French pattern, that London had or ever has had. In the large main room, with the old red plush lounges and marble tables, all the poets, writers and artists associated with the Yellow Book and the Bodley Head and kindred things, were to be seen some time during every week. Dowson, Johnson, Davidson, Phillips,

Beardsley, Leonard Smithers, Orpen ... indeed almost all the names that survive from that period had some part in the nights of the Café Royal. It was a centre for talk and discussion and argument and disagreement and accord and sometimes anger. Art meant something to those men; something to live for, fight for, and die for. None of them could be called great, but each of them was devoted and, in spite of a certain amount of pose, sincere. It was easy to laugh at them and their Quartier Latin affectations, but with those affectations they did manage to break down and destroy a lot of old English affectations, and to open the way to a new freedom for writers and artists. In that pioneering campaign the Café Royal nights were a ponderable factor.

The night-life of Leicester Square in the 'nineties was, in a slightly milder way, what the life of Haymarket had been in the 'sixties and 'seventies. What with the Empire Promenade, the Continental beer-cellars, and the various Lounges to which the street-girls were admitted with a free drink on the house, there was some justification for the attacks on it. A prominent woman in those attacks was a Mrs. Ormiston Chant, who made a big Press story with articles on The Scandal of the Empire Promenade, and received a rejoinder from the dramatic critic of the *Daily Telegraph*, Clement Scott, in an article headed Prudes on the Prowl. The subject was hotly debated in correspondence, and meetings were held; but Leicester Square remained unaffected until the war of 1914 did what the reformers had vainly tried to do. No law or authority cleaned up Leicester Square. It attended to itself. During those war years the girls just disappeared. Everybody asked—where have they gone? And the answer, when it came, was just too surprising. That soldiers' chorus of 1914—"Good-bye, Piccadilly; Farewell, Leicester Square"—said more than it knew. It marked the passing of a certain way of life and the opening of the twentieth century.

The passing of one phase of that way of life is, by some of us, regretted. The nights at Covent Garden opera. For most of the box-holders it may have been more a social than a musical function. Its system may, as some critics hold, have done opera little good by giving fabulous salaries to stars who chose to appear only in those hackneyed operas which gave the greatest display to their voices. Perhaps. But when one thinks of the thin, wan English voices we hear in opera to-day, and recalls the golden fire and passion that welled from the Covent Garden stage through the 'nineties and the first seven years of this century.... It is a matter of personal taste; of whether you prefer opera intelligently sung without much voice, or opera carelessly but magnificently sung. The English are ballad-singers, not opera-singers. They

WE WON'T GO HOME TILL MORNING

can never Let Go. My choice is for the passion and fire and volume; for Battistini, van Rooy, Maurel, Journet, and, if I had heard him—and I am told you could hear him at the far end of Long Acre—Tamagno. For Destinn and Eames and Calvé and Sembrich. And, in this century, for the king and queen of them all—Caruso and Melba.

There have been no nights at the opera to match those nights. We have had better productions, better *décor*, and a more intelligent ensemble, but still something has been missing. Team-spirit, the ideal of the present age, is a great thing. The only fault I find with it is that while I can perceive that everybody is playing splendidly for the team, they seem to have mislaid the other half of the team. Setting music aside, the front of the house on those nights presented such a scene as we are hardly likely to see again. The glow and glitter made by the horseshoe of boxes; the silk and lace; the emeralds and pearls; the tiaras and ospreys; the animation and the sense of an Occasion—it was all on a scale seen in no other English theatre. It was the last phase of Social Magnificence.

During those Grand Seasons of opera—May to July—agreeable open-air nights could be had at the Exhibitions at Earl's Court. The Earl's Court crowd was as mixed as those of Vauxhall and Ranelagh had been. Everybody went there. The illuminated gardens, the illuminated lake, the Big Wheel, the many restaurants (from one for epicures down to those for the people who thought only of roast beef), the sideshows, the fireworks, the music—those things drew all sorts and conditions. It was ... but the present generation has seen what it was at Wembley, only what they saw was five sizes larger and consequently not so agreeable. Between those two places came the White City, and when one remembers the crowds that every night through the summer flocked to those three places, one wonders why London in peace-time never had a permanent place of that kind.

Earl's Court would sometimes have special Gala Nights when decoration and illumination were more lavish. During the 'nineties it had one night, not arranged by the management, which made quite a big Fleet Street story. It also made a number of serious, respectable people, who had never before got home with the milk, do just that thing. It was the Night the Big Wheel Stuck. The Big Wheel was a very big wheel with a number of carriages suspended from its rim. A ride in one of those carriages was a good sixpenny thrill. The slow revolution of the wheel took you up and up and up, and at the topmost point gave you an immense view over day or night London. On that particular night, the illuminated Wheel was making its revolution when something went wrong with the mechanism, and it stopped. Frantic efforts were made to set it going, and to bring the passengers down, but it refused to move. Those in the upper carriages had to stay there all night. Firemen were sent up the frame of the wheel, and went from carriage to carriage with coffee and sandwiches. It was in working order again at dawn, and when the prisoners were brought down the management voluntarily and handsomely promised some little compensation to those who had been subjected to what was then thought a night of suffering and peril. Their great-grandchild, Little Audrey, would, I imagine, just laugh and laugh at their notion of suffering and peril.

Boxing was as popular an evening entertainment in the 'nineties as it has been in present times. In addition to the more or less private contests of the National Sporting Club, boxing was held at all sorts of places in London—gymnasia, halls, public-house annexes, and swimming-baths. It was even introduced as, in those days, a new attraction at music-halls, and one of my earliest recollections is of witnessing sparring bouts at the old Royal Aquarium between J. J. Corbett and Kid McCoy, and between Jim Jeffries and another whose name is lost. The most interesting home of boxing—interesting as a bizarre nocturne—was Wonderland, at Whitechapel. It was a bit of Bartholomew Fair; elemental life, elemental excitement, elemental language, elemental enjoyment. It made a fine bit of colour; ring and audience sharply divided in discs of glare and gloom, and peace and roar. The only peaceful spot really was the ring, where two men, without any of the passion of their partisans, scientifically hammered each other.

But the very effervescence of new ideas, new movements in art, the new motor-car, new pleasures, new sins, was a symptom of unease. The hilarity of those 'nineties nights, the strained efforts at "brilliance," the cultivation of perverse attitudes—it was the desperate hilarity of boredom. Nothing had happened to England for so long that life was becoming tedious. And then something did happen. By present-day standards, it was a mere incident; a series of skirmishes, or what would now be affairs of outposts, in a distant country. But it did the needful thing. It first sent the country into a frenzy of enthusiasm, and then sobered it and set it in the mood to face what was to come fifteen years later. Gaiety went on, but the tempo was reduced and the tone was lighter, and the fevered spirit of the 'nineties went into the shadows and remained there until the nineteen-twenties.

Nights of Our Own Time

*It frequently breakfasts at afternoon tea,
And dines on the following day.*

LEWIS CARROLL.

NIGHT-LIFE UNDER Edward the King was rather more seemly than it had been during the years when he was Prince. In serious circles it became less severe, and in bohemian circles it changed from loose to easy. Where there had been restraint on the one hand, and licence on the other, there was liberty. People were more natural. It was perhaps a frivolous, frou-frou age, that first decade, but its grace and lightness were welcome. Just as the 'nineties are (unreasonably) held to be represented by the *Yellow Book*, so that decade was associated with the Smart Set—a sort of fore-runner of the Bright Young Things of the nineteen-twenties. There were not many of them, but then, there were not many issues of the *Yellow Book*. But there were enough of them to draw that Press and pulpit denunciation which helped to make the name stick, and to justify the use of the term as the title of a magazine of light Society stories. They were harmless enough, and their nights were not as lurid as they liked to let it be thought. Anyway, they made things move, and with that movement life generally became simpler.

Dinner, for example. The long plethoric dinner went into the past, and its hour became later. Edward did not like sitting long at table, and where dinner had been eight or nine courses, it became, at houses that he honoured, four or five. Anything that Edward did, set the note for the next rank, and fashions and ways begun by him slowly filtered down from rank to rank; as they always do. But he had two failures with his innovations. I read somewhere a horrifying story that one of his favourite dishes was a pork chop dressed with ice-cream. That may explain his objection to a long sitting, but there are no reports of any of his subjects having loyally shortened their appetites with that dish. The other fashion that had no followers was trousers pressed at the sides. But the Edwardian age was rich in new fashions. Every year brought change.

There was change in the theatre. The light theatre, with the help of Viennese composers, became lighter. The serious theatre became more intelligent. The streets were more generously lit. The night became part of everybody's day. Soho became a favourite evening resort of the suburbs. The older restaurants, which had known so many raffish nights, either changed their note to the new conditions, or were abandoned by the public, and disappeared. Many new restaurants and new kinds of café were opened. The closing hour for bars was half-past twelve, but after-theatre suppers went on somewhat later, and clubs pleased themselves. There was no need then for the subterfuge of bottle-parties, or legal rulings as to whether a rubber sandwich constituted a "meal."

A new evening entertainment appeared about this time, but it was not known in sophisticated circles. It was patronised only by the poor and the simple. It had no elaborate plaster palaces in main streets. It was found in little derelict halls in side streets, and admission could be had for twopence and threepence. The cinematograph was then in its infancy. It has stayed there ever since.

Seaside nights had much more diversion, and more kinds of it, than those described by Dickens and Surtees. They had indeed more than has been allowed in our own time, when, under our blue laws, towns have to go dead while it is still light. In a certain extreme kind of what one may call folk-gaiety, Blackpool led and still leads. No other English resort had or has such spiritual kinship with Coney Island. (I wonder some Lancashire writer hasn't by now given us a volume of Blackpool Nights; judging by his sketches of northern life, Mr. Thompson could do it well, and from all one has heard there would be no lack of richness of material.) Southend and Margate served folk-gaiety to Londoners, but without the Coney Island crash and fire; and Brighton contrived to serve everybody with something of everything. Concert-halls and dance-halls, under the new name of Kursaal, were a feature of all the popular places, and drew crowds every night; even when, as at some summer resorts, they were perversely called Winter Gardens. Most places had gardens which were illuminated at night, and in some of them things got so loose that you were even allowed to take what is called "alcoholic refreshment" right up to eleven o'clock, while listening to the music—just as though you were in one of those dreadful Continental places. Various energetic bodies, however, stopped that moral rot, and everything in the garden is now as sober as a Trollope novel.

It was during this decade that the new kind of night-club appeared in London. It was not, like those of the 'nineties, expensive and rackety, nor was it like Evans's of the 'seventies and other large establishments of that time. It was small and simple and intimate. The first of these things was started by Mme Strindberg and Austin Harrison, who was

68 The Lights of Picadilly Circus

69 The Lights of Soho

70 The Lights of the Strand

then editing the *English Review*. It was in Heddon Street, and was named The Cave of the Golden Calf. It was intended as a conversation club, with a little occasional entertainment, a chanteur or a diseuse, on the lines of *Le Chat Noir*. It opened after the theatre, and was a place to which one could go after closing-time at the Café Royal. For a time it was the fashion. Some of the young found a new excitement in having breakfast at four in the morning—beer and eggs-and-bacon, beer and kippers, or sausages—in an atmosphere of moderns and intellectuals and Futurism. Then came more elaborate and more expensive places.

Murray's was, I believe, the first of them. Later came the Embassy, and a number of others, and the night-club, which earlier had been a rather furtive, limited, masculine affair, became generally the vogue. In the form of a smart supper and dancing club, it was a pleasure which the most respectable could enjoy. Much later, a swarm of shabby little two-room places, in West End cellars, made the term "night-club" again synonymous with the furtive and disreputable. Through the last war, and through the years between that war and this, those small, obscure places grew in number and in variety. They were not, of course, real clubs like the smart places. They had no committee, no formal election, no scrutiny of candidates' social qualifications. Their prices were high, and they offered little comfort or amenity. Most of them were just places for drinking after hours. A few of them gave some sort of entertainment in the way of singers, and a dance-floor, and a crashing and howling negroid band, but they were too small to be comfortable.

Almost every street in Soho had one or two, mostly in a basement, and almost every provincial town had one or two. They came and went like the bat. Closed in one place, they took a new name and opened in another. They spread from the West End to the suburbs, so that people living outside the centre could have a night-life of their own without making an awkward four-in-the-morning journey back.

The parents and begettors of those places were the repressive laws. When laws are made to placate a small majority, the minority will always find means of getting round them. They did so in this matter. When they were told that they should not have a drink after eleven o'clock, they said: "Won't we? We'll see about that." They found they could do it by forming a club, so clubs were formed with no other purpose than that of supplying drinks beyond the hours permitted to the public. When the clubs were harried and prosecuted for accepting members on the mat, a new means was found—the bottle-party. No sooner was that set going than authority sought means of making the bottle-party illegal. And so it goes on, and all sorts of mischiefs and abuses are created which, under full liberty to sup with a glass of wine at such hours after midnight as one pleases, would never arise. Strange how authority now, as in the fourteenth century, hates people who want to sit up late. But law or no law, they will do it. They will not go home unless they want to. If they choose to breakfast at afternoon tea, and dine on the following day, they will. They will observe all laws made in reason and common-sense; they will question all those whose point and purpose are in conflict with social liberty. The tug-of-war has been constant; on the one side the authorities, set on controlling night-life; on the other, the public, determined to have it. One set of lawyers in Parliament frames laws against it; another set of lawyers shows its clients "legal" ways of dodging those laws; and between them they make law ridiculous.

The 1914 war did not interfere with the night-life of our towns as the present war has done. There was a black-out of a sort, but only of a sort. All street-lamps were alight at night, with their glasses painted a dark-blue, so that each street seemed full of police-stations. Buses and cabs retained their lamps, just slightly dimmed, and one could get about quite easily. Shop-blinds and house-blinds had to be drawn, but not so rigidly as now, when not a half-inch gleam of the faintest glow must be seen. Shop-doors were not shrouded in maze-like contraptions of black boarding through which one has to turn and turn; if the doors were of glass they just had a curtain to them. It was such a black-out that if the young could see it in these days they would think all the lights had gone on.

Night-life, instead of being, as now, almost non-existent, was, if anything, intensified. Bars were open only from 6.30 to 9.30, but everybody was so anxious that the men of the forces should have a "good time" that—well, they did. Various ways were discovered of providing it. America, under Prohibition, discovered similar ways. The effect of that war on theatres and music-halls was the opposite of that of the present war. In London they had a boom time. It was a boom chiefly of rubbish, but while most theatres were getting full houses for facetious farces, and "girl" shows and revues, a number of intelligent young people in London were able to have their first experience of Opera Nights at Drury Lane and the Aldwych Theatre. Sir Thomas Beecham, to his great credit, offered the public a little grace to sweeten those ugly years, and gave us delightful nights of Mozart, Wagner, Moussorgsky, Verdi, and Puccini. These are still uglier years, and the few

71 Saloon Bar

72 Amusement Fair

73 Snack Bar

theatres that, at the time of writing, are still open, are doing for the most part only the light and frivolous. The alternative to the theatre—the B.B.C.—has been doing something for which the terms "light" and "frivolous" are unduly complimentary.

Restaurants, too, did well, despite "meatless days," the clipping of coupons, and the removal of drinks from the table at the hour of schoolboys' bedtime. There was no acute food-shortage, though I remember that on meatless days one or two restaurants served stewed goat, and for a short time swedes took the place of potatoes. There was no limit to the number of courses that might be served, and as there had been no exodus from the cities and towns, there was no lack of custom. Air-raids were not on the scale of those of these times, and at night everything was open and well-filled. Dress rules were generally relaxed, and in theatres and restaurants lounge suits and uniforms were more numerous than dinner-jackets. Dancing was a regular part of the programme of most restaurants. Dance-music then kept some relation to music. The jazz-band had not arrived; the waltz was still popular, and there was the fox-trot. Riot had reached no farther point than what seems now the regularity of rag-time.

If they were not the Nights of Gladness of the 1913 waltz, they were nights of steady cheerfulness. Brightness seemed a duty to "the men," and everybody was doing it. But with the end of it all, some of the young well-to-do seemed to lose their senses. In the nineteen-twenties there was much money about. Numbers of business men had done well out of the war. Their children helped them to spend it. They were not content with turning night into day. They turned it into a daze of idiot revelry. That small section—and at any time it has never been more than a small section—which stayed up all night not only expressed its high spirits in the manner expressed by an ugly and newly-imported American word, Whoopee; it tried to heighten them with drugs, and there were some tragic consequences.

It was at this time that the quarter called Mayfair was invaded by a horde of people who were not, even in the Thackeray sense, Mayfair. They took stable-lofts in mews, and turned them into flats, and followed a way of life as reckless as Becky Sharp's, and without its magnificence. The function of the day was the cocktail party, which went on to all hours. Dinner came later and later. In Early Victorian times it had been five o'clock. Then it was changed to six; then to seven; then to eight; and then half-past eight or nine; until, with the six o'clock cocktails and snacks, it was by many people omitted altogether, and the after-theatre supper took its place. It does to-day. The smarter restaurants have a fair number of tables taken for dinner, but the big crowd is the supper crowd. Lewis Carroll was a prophet.

During the rackety nineteen-twenties a number of new diversions were added to night-life. Greyhound-racing by electric light was introduced, and at once became almost as popular with the workers as football. Then came dirt-track racing in illuminated arenas, when young men risked their necks and limbs in a sport as dangerous as war, and for a time became, with the more simple kind of girl, brighter idols even than film-stars. The huge Palais de Danse arrived, with official dancing-partners who could be hired at a small fee. But this, except in size, was not new; the dance-hall had been a social institution for nearly two centuries, and in the nineteenth century both Cremorne and the Argyle Rooms had dancing-partners on hire. In the hotels a new male type appeared—the dancing-partner for women—a sleek and slim and lithe type, who was unkindly named by the French term, *gigolo*. The ice-rink, a popular diversion of the 'fifties, was revived; and a night-entertainment that was new to this country appeared in London. This was the motor-coach tour of what was called the Underworld of London. But the promoters had unaccountable ideas of where it was located. The coaches went east.

This recalls to me a misadventure of an American friend of mine in Paris. He had been taken during his first few weeks round what are called the night sights of Paris, and had been disappointed. It was all very tame. He had expected to see something out of *L'Assomoir* or *Le Ventre de Paris*, and he hadn't. He felt that there must be somewhere a much ruder and wilder night-life which visitors wouldn't hear of, and which no guide would ever reveal. Then he met a journalist on one of the popular Paris dailies, a born Parisian who knew Paris like his hand—its every street and utmost penetralia. In bad French he put his request to the journalist; would it be possible for him (the journalist) to show him some night the *real* underworld of Paris? Not what was called the underworld; not Montmartre or Belleville or the rue de Lappe or those places round the Bastille, or the catacomb cafés, but the real *under*world, which visitors never saw.

The journalist listened courteously, and, after getting the request repeated, signified that he understood well what the American desired. When asked if it could be done, he said But Certainly. It would arrange itself most easily, and he would be charmed to be of service. Let M'sieu' present himself at the Porte St. Denis next Monday at midnight, when the journalist would be at liberty. To wear, of course, the old clothes—understood. A revolver? Ah, but no. Not at all necessary. But the old clothes—yes.

My friend kept the appointment. Up came the journalist with another man, a shabby working-man. They went down a side-street bordered by a high wall. At one point of the wall was a black door. The shabby man produced a key and unlocked it. My friend saw a dark flight of stone steps. The journalist said: *"Prenez garde!"* My friend, with a slight spasm of funk and a little thrill at what he would have to tell (if he came out alive) prepared himself for anything.

Then, with a pocket-torch, the journalist lighted him down the slippery steps, and took him for an hour's walk through the real underworld of Paris—the Paris sewers.

The London night was brightened about this time by a new kind of coffee-stall—bigger and better, on the line of the American midnight "lunch-waggon." Some of these had a trailer in which were a table and seats for six or eight people. All-night snack-bars appeared here and there, and one or two of the popular Corner Houses kept open all night. Nobody in those days seemed to have any care or any need of the knitter-up of the ravelled sleeve. Young people were so eager to make up for lost living that they were not willing to spend a quarter of their lives in unconsciousness; though in fact many of them spent more than that in a sort of walking daze. As the man who is never really sober is never really drunk, so they who did not sleep were seldom ever really awake.

A night sport devised by the over-monied, under-minded Bright Young Things was the Treasure Hunt. But it was not new. It had been first used years before by Sir George Newnes as a competition in one of his popular weeklies. It was a sort of detective game. You started from a central place and were led by clues, genuine or false, from point to point, until you arrived at the winning-post, which might be miles away from London. Another form was that by which the players were sent out at night to collect a list of incongruous objects—a marmoset, a copy of a particular book, a public notice (such as "Keep to the Left"), the wine-list of a particular restaurant, a couple of nutmegs, a pork pie, a packet of hair-pins, and so on. The winner was he or she who made the collection in the shortest time.

Folly is of no one age. It flourished before Erasmus, and ever since his celebration of it, it has been the idol of all fools, rich and poor. Mainly, of course, of the rich since they have both greater leisure and greater means of making offerings to it. It is an indifferent substitute for joy, but there was not much joy in the air of the nineteen-twenties.

There was rather a sort of exasperated indulgence in any kind of crude fun. The war had ended but there was no peace. It seemed to be half-guessed that it was a period merely of marking time for the next disaster. They gathered roses, if only paper roses, while they might. They were bored. There was a phrase commonly heard among ex-Army men, both officers and privates—"Roll on, the next war." They are now middle-aged, and they have it. They are no longer bored. They are indeed giving a good account of themselves.

The folly was, as I said, confined to a small section; that vociferous section that manages to get "in the news" and will do anything to get there. The sensible majority went on in its usual way, taking its amusement rationally and decently, and making a night in town a pleasure rather than a paroxysm.

Restaurant-cabaret, which is still the vogue, really came in with the nineteen-twenties. It was not the casual cheap cabaret of Paris: it was a "luxury restaurant" affair, and its model was the sophisticated and elaborately dressed (or undressed) floor-show of America. Which led purists to protest against the misuse of the term Cabaret. Whatever term it deserved (and I can think of a few) it was instantly popular with everybody except gourmets. A few good restaurants sufficiently respected their cuisine and their patrons to have nothing to do with that noisy and vapid intrusion on the ceremony of dining or supping. They advertised, as a point in their favour, No Music, No Entertainment. But most of the smart places gave the open-mouthed public what it seemed to want.

This brought a new kind of entertainer on to the night scene. Not an actor, or a music-hall comedian, or a concert artist, but one whose technique was adapted to a dining-room. The male and female crooner, or moaner, began to trouble the night air. Their music was "blue," and their songs were called "torch" songs, which meant perhaps that they had more smoke than flame, or more words than meaning. The new Gibberish was the fashion in both popular song and serious literature. It was night-time in Italy when it was Wednesday over here, and lack of bananas called for negative affirmation. "Craziness" in entertainment, which began in those days, is still the general note to-day. Nothing must mean anything—a reflection, no doubt, of the general life of this age. Bat's wings, bat's eyes, and bat's brains.

In the nineteen-thirties night-life began to move out of the cities and towns. The road-house—another American importation—became the fashion. It gave an excuse for a car-run twenty or thirty miles out, and it offered dance-band, entertainers, grill-room, snack-bar, and Ye

74 Music-hall

75 Intimate Cabaret

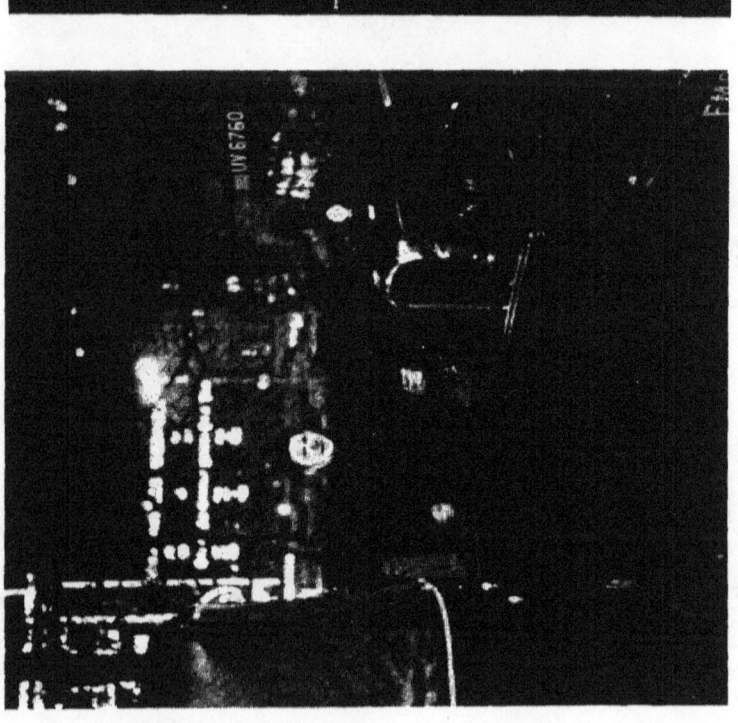

76 Street Entertainer, Leicester Square   77 Night on the Embankment

Olde Cocktayle Barre. In summer it offered the swimming-bath, which somehow escaped being called Ye Nue. One or two of the most modern places—concrete outside, and panelled inside with Ye Olde Oake—offered landing-ground for private planes. Up to the outbreak of war those places, almost any night of any season, had full houses—and several still do. It was a way of having a night in town in the country; because, however Arcadian the situation of the place might be, once you entered the doors you were back in Shaftesbury Avenue or Coventry Street. It gave you the feeling of one of those dreams in which you are in two places at once. You could sit in a Jermyn Street snack-bar, and through the window, fifty yards away, you saw the moonlit countryside.

A development from the road-house was the country night-club. In the London area these were most numerous in that reach of the Thames where are Taplow and Maidenhead and Bray. Maidenhead, with its long theatrical associations, was made the centre—indeed, the vortex—of a certain jazz kind of night-life. The original clubs were real clubs, decent and orderly; but when their success was noted, a group of less agreeable clubs of the Soho kind sprang up, until the night steamed with noise, and the quiet residents at last revolted against the bad name their town was getting, and the way it was getting it, and something was done to clear out the undesirables.

One of the earliest of the better kind of riverside place was an island pleasure-garden, restaurant, dance-hall, and other attractions, in midstream at Hampton Court. This was Fred Karno's Karsino, a favourite resort of Londoners on summer nights. Those with cars could be taken across to it without leaving the car, and could have dinner or supper or a snack, and dance to one of the best bands, in the semi-open. It provided a continuation of a custom of the middle nineteenth century, when young men would tool their drags down to Richmond, with one or two "fair friends," sup at the Star and Garter, and drive back in the cool of early morning. Another custom, that of spending the night *down* the river, has passed into oblivion. But in Victorian times parties would be formed to go by boat to Greenwich or Blackwall, and take at one of the hotels the famous Whitebait Dinner (nine courses of fish with whitebait at the centre) and return by moonlight. At North Woolwich was a well-known pleasure-garden to which boats ran every summer night, and once or twice a week there were moonlight excursions from London Bridge to Rosherville. Those diversions are now of the past.

But one feature of the London nights of Victoria has been successfully revived—the old Evans's. Mr. Harold Scott, I believe, first revived it under the name of the Cave of Harmony. Later it has been known as Ridgway's Late Joys. One sits at tables, and beer and hot-dogs are served. There is a Chairman to announce the turns, and the entertainment consists of songs and recitations of the middle and later Victorian times, delivered gravely and sentimentally in contemporary costume. Songs frequently called for are *Mrs. Dyer, the Baby Farmer; Not for Joe; Don't Sell No More Beer to my Father; Polly Perkins; In the Gloaming;* and *The Ballad of Sam Hall.* In ordinary times it opened at eleven and went on till about two, but under war conditions it begins at nine. It was an interesting experiment, and was successful from the start. It is at once old and new, and it makes a pleasant relief from the "craziness" of modern music-hall and film.

This craziness got into one or two restaurants. There is no arguing about tastes in pleasure, but it is odd that people should have found dinner or supper more delightful because a man went helter-skelter round the restaurant on roller-skates, weaving between tables and skimming round the waiters. Or because somebody picked their pockets. Or because a man conducted the band by walking about on his hands and waving his legs. Or because people at other tables threw things at them. But juvenility persists long in the English, as with their life-long harping on their schools; and it may be that this delight in disordered meals is a reaction from the prohibitions of childhood. Meals in the nursery had to be taken decorously. Now at last the restaurateur gives them the chance of releasing all that years ago had to be repressed.

Under the long black night which began in September 1939, and still endures, and with the arduous duties imposed upon or assumed by the bulk of those who peopled the normal night-scene, little night-life has been possible. At least, little festive night-life. Night-life of a queer kind, and a new kind, we have certainly experienced. Many people who never before stayed out all night have often fulfilled the burden of the old song—"Till daylight doth appear." The dark hours, once given to relaxation, have been the stern part of our day, and though men on leave, and others whose hours were free, have dined and danced, and night-clubs have kept open, the night-life of cities in the danger areas has been only of a dim, subdued kind. In the "safer areas," it goes on much as usual and on the surface, and at road-houses anywhere near a camp it is of the old and hearty kind; but generally it has been restrained.

78, 79 Covent Garden Nocturnes

80 A Concert for Tube Shelterers, 1941

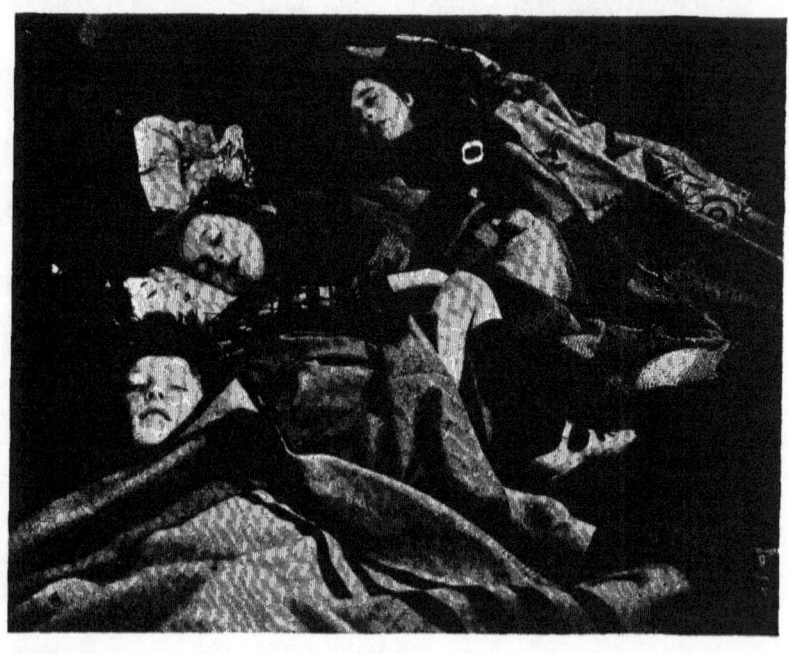

81 Bedtime, 1941

The lig..ter evenings brought a lighter spirit, and enabled the theatres re-open at night, and many restaurants which had not been open for nner iring the winter returned to their old habits and kept open till at least midnight; but all through the dark evenings the night-life that persisted went on in what that Paris journalist would have called the real under-the-world. It went on in re-inforced, shored-up basements of hotels and restaurants. Most places in their advertising have made a point of stating that the ball-room is so many feet below the surface. There has been a revival of the beer-cellar of the 'nineties. The roof-garden has been used for other purposes, and vaults have been turned into boudoirs and bedrooms. Midnight parties have been given in caves under the cliffs. Song-and-dance have been heard and seen in places once known only to the coal-man and the pantry-boy.

London's Underground system was taken by the people for their own shelter. In the original sulphuric Underground Railway Sir Lewis Morris (appropriately at that time) wrote his forgotten *Epic of Hades*; and from all one can hear, the stations have been a setting for a night-life which might have provided Sir Lewis with more material. It seems to have been a mixture of mouth-organ, lecture, educational talk, scenes from Shakespeare by theatre-groups, halfpenny nap, find-the-lady, community singing, and snores.

But there were still those imperturbable spirits who preferred amusement on the surface, in any conditions of peril, and somehow managed to get it, if only in a humble way. The bars, amid bombs and barrage, have been well filled, and darts have been played in the din. Song-parties have gone wandering about the streets, with shell splinters dropping around them. Snack-bars and milk-bars have kept open at all hours. Even street-organs have played. On four raid nights of last winter, at nine o'clock, when, on each occasion, the attack was most fierce, some glorious and unconquerable grinder brought his organ into the road where I live, and ground out *Sons of the Sea*, *Alexander's Ragtime Band*, and other old stuff. This adaptation to extraordinary conditions was noticed by Sir Philip Game in his annual Police report. Familiarity, he said, was breeding a certain contempt for night bombing, and the demand for night entertainment after dark was again on the increase.

It always was and always will be, whatever the conditions. From the earliest times people of a certain temperament have been willing to go anywhere at night except home. Neither laws nor the after-dark dangers of prowling ruffians (which, up to the late seventeenth century, were real dangers) could stop them. We are living now in worse conditions. We have the darkness and another kind of danger, and yet, where regular night-life has been suspended, we have, as they had, a substitute of the irregular. Our night-scene has other correspondences with theirs. Where the link-man with his flaming torch lit people from carriage to door, we are now lit by the commissionaire with his electric torch. Where the night-watchman patrolled the streets or sat in his box, we have the warden. Where the Roman sentry paced the city walls or the keep, the fire-watcher paces the roof. Where the night used to hear the watchman's cry of "Past one o'clock and a stormy night!" it now hears a cry as standardised as his; a cry that must, like his, have been uttered some thousands of times in the dark: "Put that light out!"

But light or dark, the Midnight Sons will be out. The recreations of the day-time, even if they are free to enjoy them, have no relish for them. They come fully awake only after sunset, in the bright lights. Meantime, they carry on the spirit of the town and of night, in whatever way is available, until the bright lights come again, and new diversions are devised or the old brought up in new form. There are no more Rickety-Rackety Crews, no more Jolly Good Boys, making night a tumult; and the fever of the post-war nineteen-twenties is hardly likely to recur. The quiet night-life of the war period may set a new note, and public night-life of the future may keep that note. Or it may not.

Index

(The numerals in italics denote the *figure numbers* of illustrations)

Aberdeen, Lord, 103
Addison, 23, 25
Alexander's Feast, 64
Alfred, the, 90
Alhambra, the, 106, 117, 125
Alken, H., *38, 39*
Almack's, 41f., 70, 71, 79f.
Alvanley, Lord, 74
Anacreontic Club, the, 50
Angelo, Harry, 59f., 63, 71, 80
Anguish, Mayor of Norwich, 13
Annals (Howes), 13
Apollo Gardens, 59
Apollo Room, the, 15
Apperley, C. J. (Nimrod), 101
Argyle Rooms, 138
Argyll, Duke of, 56
Arne, Dr., 49
Art of Cookery, The, 72
Arthur's, 78
Ashton, John, 21, 67
Astley, Philip, 64, 65
Astley's Amphitheatre, *36*
As You Like It, 65
Athenaeum, the, 96
Augustan Age, 24
Autobiography (Haydon), 83

Bacon (quoted), 11
Bagnigge Wells, 45, 59
Bagnios, 26, 49
Ball, The, 7
Ballet, the, *35*, 125
Bannister, Jack, 81, 86
Banquet in Presence Chamber, Hampton Court, *4*
Barron's Oyster Rooms, 119
Barrymore, Lord, 59, 61f., 66, 70
Bas-Bleu, 56
Bath, 29, *32, 33*, 33, 88
Bazaar, the, 38
B.B.C. the, 137
Beardsley, 130
Beating the Watch, 16
Beauclerk, Topham, 54, 55
Beaumont, 11
Beaux' Stratagem, The, 65
Bedford Coffee House, 48
Bedford, Duchess of, 42
Beecham, Sir Thomas, 136
Beef Steak Club, the, 68
Belcher, 89
Belle assemblée, the, 38
Belsize House, 45
Benckendorff, Count, 74
Bentley, Richard, 38
Berkeley, the, 122
Betty, Master William, 86f.
Bidford, 8
Binstead, Arthur, 127
Black-out, the, 136
Blackwall, 141

Blessington, Lady, 102
Blue Posts, 119, 125
Bluestocking Clubs, 56f.
Boat Race Night, 126
Boating, 19
Bodley Head, The, 129
Bohemian life, 127f.
Boodle's, 78, 90
Booth, Junius, 84
Boscawen, Hon. Mrs., 57
Boswell, 43, 53f., 63
Bow Street men, 92
Bowls, game of, 18
Boxing, 132
Braham, 81
Breton, Nicholas, 2
Bright Young Things, 133, 139
Brighthelmstone, 34
Brighton Pavilion, 66
Bristol, 31f., 33, 34
Britton, Thomas, 20
Brook's, *38*, 42, 66, 78, 90
Brothels, 50, 94
Brougham, Lord, 56, 103
"Brown Dozen of Drunkards" (1648), 9
Bruisers, 40
Brummell, George, 74
Buckinghamshire, Lady Albina, 60
Bunbury, H., *29, 30*
Burke, 55
Burmese, the, 119
Burney, Charles, 55
Burney, E. F., 37
Burney, Fanny, 37, 38, 40, 57
Burney, Richard, 37, 53
Burton, Robert, 16
Bush Inn, the, 60
Byron, Lord, 58f.
Byron, George Gordon, Lord, 71, 77f., 82

Cabaret, 75, 140
Café Régence, 120
Café Riche, 120
Café Royal, 120, 129f., 135
Campanology, 6f.
Campbell, 102
Canaletto, 19
Canterbury, the, 105, 122, 123, 124
Carey, Henry, 81
Carlisle, Earl of, 56
Carlton House, 66, 71
Carlton, the, 96, 122
Carlisle House, Soho, *17*
Carlyle, 110
Caroline, Princess, 68
Carroll, Lewis (quoted), 133, 137
Carter, Elizabeth, 57
Castlereagh, Lady, 79
"Cave of Harmony," the, 92, 142
Cave of the Golden Calf, the, 135
Celestial Bed, the, 63

Champion, Harry, 125
Chant, Mrs. Ormiston, 130
Chapman, 7
Charles I, King, 11
Charles II, King, 17f.
Charlotte, Princess, 68
Chaworth, Mr., 58f.
Chettle, 13
Chorus Ladies, 127
Chrysal, or the Adventures of a Guinea, 52
Chudleigh, Elizabeth, 40
Churchill, 49, 51
Cibber, Charlotte, 31f.
Cinematograph, the, 134
Circus, the, 64
Citizen of the World, 44
City Club, the, 55
Clarence, Duke of, 103
Clarendon, Lord, 56
Club Life of London, 24
Club, The, 25
Clubs, 21, 24f., 96f.
Coal Hole, the, 80, 92, 107
Coates, Robert, 87f.
Cockpit, the, *13*, 17
Cocktail parties, 137
Cocoa Tree, the, 90
Coffee House, the, 21
Coffee-stalls, 139
Coldbath Fields, 46
Coleridge, 110
Collins, William, 49
Colman, George, 73
Cooke, G. F., 86
Corbett, J. J., 132
Corinthianism, 66, 70
Cork, Countess of, 56
Cornelys, Mrs., 40f.
Cornelys Rooms, 43
Corner Houses, 139
"Countryman in London," the, *43*
Country Clubs, 141
Country parties, 112f.
Country Worker's Night Life, *29*, 35
Covent Garden, 49, 51, 60, 78, 79, 84, 87, 94, 111
Cowper, Lady, 79
Cremorne Gardens, *61*, 107, 110, 111, 138
Cribb, Tom, 82
Cripplegate, 61, 66
Criterion Long Bar, 125
Crockford's, 90, 91, 98
Crooner, the, 140
Cruikshank, George, *47*, *48*, 49, *51*, *52*, 95
Cruikshank, Robert, *42*, *43*, *44*, 95
Cumberland, Duke of, 66
Cuper's Gardens, 45
Cyder Cellar, the, 50, 92, 94, 107
Cyprians, the, 73

Daily Advertiser, the, 46
Daily Telegraph, the, 115, 130

Dance-halls, 110, 113f.
Dancing, *37*
Dashwood, Sir Francis, 52
Davidson, John, 125, 129
Debate, the, 10f., 117
Dekker, *Seven Deadly Sinnes*, 13
Delaney, Mrs., 57
Denmark, King of, 12
Devil, the, 55
Devonshire, the, 90
Devonshire, the Duke of, 41
Dibdin, Charles, 65, 81
Dickens, Charles, 92, 96, 100, 102, 109, 114
Dirt-track Racing, 138
Disher, Willson, 116
Disraeli, 90, 102
Doddington, Bubb, 52
Dog and Duck, the, 45, 59
Domestic evening amusements, 16, 121
Doré, G., *57*
d'Orleans, Duc, 103
D'Orsay, *45*, 90, 102
Dowson, 129
Drama Clubs, 59
Dram Shop, The, *41*
"Dressing for the Ball," *18*
Drum, the, 38, 39
Drury Lane, 60, 84, 87, 94
Du Maurier, 66, 67, 121

Earl's Court, 131f.
"Early Morning," by Hogarth, *23*
Earth-bathing, 63
Eccentric, the, 127
Edward VII, King, 133
Edward, Prince of Wales, 121
Egan, Pierce, 95
Eighteenth-century London Night Haunt, 50
Eighteenth-century Theatre Interior, 28
Elizabeth, Princess, 13
Elizabeth, Queen, 6, 11
Elizabethan "Stag Party," *6*
Elliston, 75, 81, 85, 86
Embankment, the, 77
Embassy, the, 135
Emma, 78
Empire, the, 117, 125
Empire Promenade, the, *64*, 130
English Review, The, 135
English Spy, 121
Epic of Hades, 143
Epsom, 33
Escoffier, 122
Essex Head Club, the (see under Sam's)
Esterhazy, 90
Esterhazy, Princess, 79
Euphues and his England, Lyly, 10
Evans, 94, 142
Evelyn, John, 18
Evenings at Home, 10
Evening Entertainments, *42*, *43*, *44*, *47*, *48*, *49*, 60, *61*, 66, *67*, 117

INDEX

Falmouth, 77
Faraday, 110
Farquhar (quoted), 23
Fauna of Iceland, The, 2
Fenton, Lavinia, 51
Fielding, Henry, 36, 49
Fifteenth-century Court Soirée, 2
Fifteenth-century Mummers, *3*
Fiera in mascherata, 38
Finish, the, 94
Fireside Conversation, 1601, Mark Twain, 11
Fireworks, 13, 40
Fitzgerald, 112
Fitzherbert, Mrs., 66f.
Fitzroy, Mrs., 42
Fladong's, 79
Florizel's Folly, 67
Folk-Lore Society, 125
Foote, Sam, 49
Forster, 109
Fox, Charles James, 55, 66
Francatelli, 122
Fuller, 11
Fun Fair, 72

Game, Sir Phillip, 143
Games in Stuart times, 18
Gaming, 3, 4, 17, 30, *45*, *46*, 49, *63*, 78, 89, 90f.
Gaming Houses, 3, *21*, *24*, 38
Garrick, 49, 54, 55, 96
Garrick's Head, the, 108
Garth, 51
Gay (quoted), 26
George III, King, 66
Gibbon, 55
Gigolo, the, 138
Gilray, James, *34*, 80
Gin Shop, the, *52*, *56*
Glenelg, Lord, 56
Goldsmith, Oliver, 43, 49, 55, *58*
Goodman's Fields Theatre, 64
Gore House, 102
Gore, Mrs., 99
Graham, Dr., 62
Grammont, 18
Grattan, 103
Great War, the, 130, 135, 136
Greaves, Samuel, 55
Greene, 13
Greenwich, 141
Greenwood, James, 114f.
Greyhound racing, 138
Grillon's, 79
Gronow, 66, 70, 72, 79, 88, 90, 91
Groom-Porter, the, 17
Grote, George, 56
Guilds, 2

Hallam, 56
Halston, 100
Hamilton, Anthony, 18
Hamilton, Duchess of, 41

Hampstead Assembly, the, 39
Hampton Court, *4*, 141
Handel, 20
Hanger, Colonel George, 66
Harp Tavern, the, 81
Harrington, Sir John, 12
Harrison, Austin, 134
Harrogate, 34
Hawkins, Sir John, 55, 57
Haydon, 83
Haymarket, *58*, 64, 94, 119
Hazlitt, 110
Hell-Fire Clubs, 52
Hell-Gate, 61, 66
Henderson, 63f.
Henry IV, reign of, 1
Henry VIII, 4
Hentzner, 5
"He Revels," Hogarth, *10*
Hertford, Lady, 41
Hertford, Lord, 73
Heywood, Thomas, 11, 16
Hogarth, Wm., *10*, *11*, *12*, *13*, *14*, *22*, *23*, *48*, *49*, 51
Holland, Lady, 102
Holland House, 71, 102
Hood, Thomas, 98, 104
Hook, Theodore, 97, 102
Hotels, 79
Hotten, J. L., 95
Houses of Assignation, 1, 3
Humbug Club, the, 50
Hummums, 49
Humphrey Clinker, 34
Hunt, Leigh, 12
Huysmans, 53

Ibbetson's, 79
Ice-Rink, the, 138
Illegal sporting events, 116
In a Music Hall, 125
Inns of Court, 6
Interludes, 6
Irving, Washington, 102
Ivy Lane Club, 55

Jackson, 89
Jacob's Well, 59f.
James I, King, 11-12
Jeffries, Jim, 132
Jeffrey, Lord, 103
Jerrold, Douglas, 109
Jersey, Lady, 79
Jersey, Lord, 80
Jerusalem Passage, 20
John Gilpin, 63
Johnson, Dr. Samuel, 43, 53f., 63
Johnson's, 114
Johnstone, Charles, 52f.
Jones, Inigo, 11, 18
Jonson, Ben, 11, 15
Jorrock's Jaunts, 53, 54, 99
Joseph Andrews, 36
Journal to Stella, 23

Journey to London, A, 23
Joyce, James, 109
Judge and Jury trials, 107
Karsino, Fred Karno's, 141
Kean, Edmund, 81f., 84f.
Keepsakes, 102
Kemble, 84
Kipling, 132
Kitchener, Dr., 72
Kursaal, the, 134

Là-bas, 53
Labourie, 76
Lads of the Fancy, 69
Lady of Pleasure, 16
Lamb, Charles, 98
Lamb, Hon. George, 75
Lami, E., 60
Landor, 102
Langton, Bennet, 54, 55
Laroon, M., 8
Late-Georgian Nocturne, A, 28
Laughing Audience, The, *11*
Le Sage, 115
Lecture, the, 110
Leges Conviviales, 15
Leicester Square, 76, 126, 130
Lennox, Charlotte, 55
Les Six, 12
Licensing laws, 120, 134, 135
Lieven, Lady, 79
Life and Career of Palmer, 110
Life in London, 95
Life of Byron, 78
Life of Edmund Kean, 81
Life of John Mytton, 101
Life of Wolsey, 3
Limmer's, 79
Liston, 81
Literary Club, the, 55f.
Lloyd, Miss, 42
Lloyd, Robert, 52
London Coffee-house, *30*
London in the Sixties, 120
London Society, 116
Long Acre, 94
Long's, 79
Lottery, the, 7
Lyceum, the, 64
Lyme Regis, 76
Lyndhurst, Lord, 103
Lyttleton, Lord, 57
Lytton, Bulwer, 90, 102

McCall, Mr., 42
McCoy, Kid, 132
Macaulay, 56, 103
Macbeth, 65
Macready, 84, 86
Magic and Mystery, 117
Maison Dorée, the, 118
Making a Night of It, 96
Man-and-Dog Fight, 115
Manneduke, Dr. de, 62

Margate Hoy, the, 62
Marquis, Don, 99
Marylebone Gardens, 39, 45
Masked Ball, the, *12*
Masquerade, the, 38
Masques, 2, 11f.
May, Phil, 127f.
Mayfair, 137
Medieval Dances, 2
Medmenham, Monks of, 52f.
Melo-Drama, 65
Melton Mowbray, 76
Mermaid, the, 11
Metternich, 103
Meurigy's, 120
Meynell, Mrs., 42
Midnight Modern Conversation, A, *14*
Minchinhampton, 33
Minstrels, 2
Moll King's Coffee-house, 48
Molloy, Fitzgerald, 81
Molyneux, Lady, 42
Monckton, Miss, 56f.
Montague, Elizabeth, 57
Montague, Lady, 34
Moore, John, 50
Moore, Tom, 71, 78, 89, 103
Moore and Burgess, minstrels, 117
More, Hannah, 56
Morning, 48
Morning After, The, *31*
Morning Post, the, 67
Morris, Captain, 50
Morris, Sir Lewis, 143
Morrow, George, 125
Motor-coach tours, 138
Mug-House, the, 24
Mummers, 2
Munden, 86
Murphy, Arthur, 49
Murray's, 135
Music clubs, 20, 59
Musical Evenings, *8, 34*
Music Halls, 74, 92, 104f., 116f., 122f., 136
Musical Small-Coal Man, the, 20
Mysteries and Moralities, 6
Mytton, Jack, 100f.

"Nag's Head," the, Clerkenwell, 107
Napoleon, Louis, 102
Nash, Beau, 29f.
Nash, Joseph, 4, 7
Nashe, 13
National Sporting Club, the, 94, 127, 132
Neville, Sir Edward, 5
Newgate, 61
Newnes, Sir George, 139
Nicholson, Renton, 51, 107
"Night," by Hogarth, *22*
Night Club, the, 40, 134f.
Nineteenth-century Public-house, 93
"Nineties," the, 124f.
Norfolk, Duke of, 67f.
North Woolwich, 141

INDEX

Northumberland, Duchess of, 41
Nottinghamshire Club, the, 58

Offley's, 93
O.P. Riots, 84
Opera, the, 38, 39, 59, 130f., 136
Opium Rooms, the, 57, 114
Orange Girl, the, 29
Ord, Mrs., 57
Oriental, the, 96
Original, 98
Orpen, 130
Overstone, Lord, 56
Oxberry, 81, 82
Oxford and Cambridge, the, 96

Palace, the, 117
Palais de Danse, 138
Pall Mall, 96
Palmerston, Lord, 74
Pantheon, the, 20, 41, 43
Panton Street Rooms, the, 39
Paris Underworld, 138f.
Pasqua Rosee's, 21
Pelham, Miss, 42
Pelican Club, the, 127
Pembroke, Lady, 41, 42
Penny Gaff, the, 83
Penny Reading, the, 118
Pepuschi, 20
Pepys, Samuel, 17, 20
Pepys, Sir William, 57
Peregrine Pickle, 35
Phillips, 129
Phillip's New Wells, 46
Piazzas, the, 49
Piccadilly, *68*, 96, 126
Piccadilly Saloon, the, 119
Pickwick, 95f.
Pic-Nic Society, the, 60f.
Pope, 23
Porson, Richard, 50
Post and Pair, 3
Post-War Nights, 136
Present-day Night-life, 136f.
Potteries, the, 115f.
Prince Regent, the, 65f., 71
Prior, Mathew, 20
"Pub-Crawl," the, 47
Public House, the, 71
Puckle, James, 25
Pugin, *20*
Punch, 111, 125

Queen's Birthday Ball, 40
Queen's Head, the, 59
Quin, 49

Random, Roderick, 47f.
Ranelagh, *15*, *19*, 39, 40, 43, 45
Ratcliff Highway, the, 114
Reading, the, 109f.
Real Life in London, 95
Recessional, 3

Reform, the, 96
Regency Buck, the, *39*
Regency period, the, *70*
Reich, Emil, 62
Relapse, The, 22
Reminiscences of Henry Angelo, 59
Restaurants, 26, 118f., 134, 137f., 142
Return from the Tythe Feast (1829), (*frontispiece*), *1*
Reynolds, Joshua, 55, 57
Rhodes, the Singing Collier, 81
Richardson, 27
Richmond, Duke of, 41
Ridgeways Late Joys, 142
Ridotto, the, 38f.
Ring, the, 89
Ritz, M., 122
River pageants, 19
Road-House, the, 141
Rogers, 98
Romano's, 127
Romeo and Juliet, 87f.
Rosherville, 141
Rouget's, 120
Rout, the, 39
Rowe, Nicholas, 29
Rowlandson, T., *16*, *18*, *20*, *31*, *35*, *36*, *40*, *41*, 80
Royalt', Theatre, 64
Royal Equestrian Philharmonic, the, 65
Ruskin, 11
Russell, Earl, 56
Russell, Lord John, 103

Sadler's Wells, 45, 64
St. James' Bar, 125
St. James' Day, 51
Sala, *Twice Round the Clock*, 58, 59
Sally in our Alley, 81
Sam's, 55
Sandwich, Earl of, 52
Savage, the, 127
Savoy, the, 122
Scarborough, 34
Scott, Clement, 130
Seaside nights, 99, 134
Secret History of the Court of James I, 12
Sedley, Sir Charles, 58
Sefton, Lady, 79
Seventeenth-century Bachelor Party, 8
Seventeenth-century Concert, 9
Seventeenth-century Tavern Scene, 14
Shakespeare, 4, 7f.
Shallow, 1
Sheridan, Thomas, 63f.
Sheridan, Tom, 77
Sheridan, R. B., 55
Shilling Hop, the, 110
Shirley, James, 11, 16, 18
Siddons, Sarah, 86
Silver Hells, 91
Sir John Oldcastle, the, 46
Sixteenth-century Concert, 6
Sixteenth-century Gaming-house, 4

Sixteenth-century Torchlight Procession, 5
Sketches by Boz, 92
Smart Set, the, 133
Smith, Adam, 55
Smith, Albert, 109
Smith, J. R., 17
Smith, James and Horace, 102
Smith, Sydney, 103
Smithers, Leonard, 130
Smollett, 34
Smyrna Coffee House, the, 25
Snack Bar, the, 73
Society of Cogers, 51
Society of Good Fellows, the, 92
Soho, 40, 69, 134, 135
Song and Supper Rooms, 92
Sons of Ben, 15
Spectator, The, 26, 29
Spence, 23
Spiller, James, 51
Spiller's Head, the, 51
Spring, Tom, 89
Spring Garden, 21
Stael, Mme de, 103
Stanhope, Lady, 41
Stanhope, Lord, 56
Stanley, Lord, 56
Staple of News, The, 15f.
Star and Garter, the, 141
Steele, Dick, 32
Steven's Hotel, 78
Stewart, Frances, 19
Stillingfleet, 56
Strand, the, 70, 126f.
Stratford, 8
Street Clubs, 24
Strindberg, Mme, 134
Sublime Free and Easy, the, 92
Supper cabaret, 92
Surrey Theatre, the, 65
Surtees, 92, 99, 112
Sussex, Royal Duke of, 71
Swell's Night Guide, The, 108
Swift, Jonathan, 23
Sybil, 105
Symons, Arthur, 125

Table customs, 71f.
Talleyrand, 90, 103
Tavern, the, 1, 3, 6, 14f., 25, 27, 79, 80f., 93
Temple of Apollo, 45
Temple of Flora, 45
Temple of Health, 62
Thackeray, 102, 109
Thatched House Tavern, 71
Theatre, the, 6, 21, 25, 27f., 30f., 62, 64f., 65, 83f., 104, 127, 133, 136
Theatres of Variety, 92
Thrale, 55
Thompson, Mr., 134

Thurlow, Lord, 103
Timbs, John, 24
Traveller's, the, 90
Travelling entertainment, 3
Treasure Hunt, 139
Trocadero Bar, 128
Tube Shelterers, 1941, *80*, *81*
Tunbridge Walks, 34
Tunbridge Wells, 30, 33
Twelfth Night, 18
Twelfth Night, 8f.

Ude, 90
Union, the, 96
Universities, 6
University Club, the, 96

Vanbrugh (quoted), 23
Vauxhall, New Gardens, *16*, 21, 39f., 43, 45, 61, 110
Verrey's, 122
Vesey, Mrs., 57
Victorian Intemperance, *51*
Village Assembly, 37
Vine Street, 126

Walker, Thomas, 98
Walpole, Horace, 34, 38f., 57
Ward, Hon. George, 74
Ward, Ned, 30
Wartime pleasures, 143
Watering-places, 99f.
Watier's, 76, 78, 90
Wellington, Duke of, 80, 90
Wembley Exhibition, 131
Westmacott, Charles, 73, 89, 93, 95
Wharton, Duke of, 51, 52
White City, the, 131
White Conduit House, 45
Whitebait dinner, the, 141
White's, 42, 78, 79, 90
Wide-Awake Club, the, 92
Wigstead, H., 28
Wilkie, 83
Wilkes, John, 51, 52
William III, King, 22
Willis' Rooms, 42, 111
Wilson, Harriete, 71f., 100
Wilson Sisters, 73f.
Winkles and Champagne, 116
Winter Gardens, 134
Wise Woman of Hogsdon, 16
Wolsey, Cardinal, 3f.
Wolves Club, the, 81
Wonderland, Whitechapel, 132
Worcester, 37
Wyndham, the, 96

Yellow Book, The, 129, 133
York Place, Whitehall, 3
Yule Log, at Penshurst, the, 7